A PRESCRIPTION FOR LIVING WITH PURPOSE

A PRESCRIPTION FOR
LIVING
WITH
PURPOSE

Maintaining Hope, Healing, and
Connection as You Create the Life
You Were Destined to Live

ADAM MEADOWS, MD

NEW YORK

LONDON • NASHVILLE • MELBOURNE • VANCOUVER

A Prescription for Living with Purpose

Maintaining Hope, Healing and Connection as You Create the Life You Were Destined to Live

Published in New York, New York, by Morgan James Publishing. Morgan James is a trademark of Morgan James, LLC. www.MorganJamesPublishing.com

ISBN 9781642798494 paperback
ISBN 9781642798500 eBook
Library of Congress Control Number: 2019919229

Cover Design by:
Rachel Lopez
www.r2cdesign.com

Interior Design by:
Christopher Kirk
www.GFSstudio.com

Morgan James is a proud partner of Habitat for Humanity Peninsula and Greater Williamsburg. Partners in building since 2006.

Get involved today! Visit
MorganJamesPublishing.com/giving-back

A PRESCRIPTION FOR
LIVING
WITH
PURPOSE

Maintaining Hope, Healing, and
Connection as You Create the Life
You Were Destined to Live

ADAM MEADOWS, MD

NEW YORK

LONDON • NASHVILLE • MELBOURNE • VANCOUVER

A Prescription for Living with Purpose

Maintaining Hope, Healing and Connection as You Create the Life You Were Destined to Live

Published in New York, New York, by Morgan James Publishing. Morgan James is a trademark of Morgan James, LLC. www.MorganJamesPublishing.com

ISBN 9781642798494 paperback
ISBN 9781642798500 eBook
Library of Congress Control Number: 2019919229

Cover Design by:
Rachel Lopez
www.r2cdesign.com

Interior Design by:
Christopher Kirk
www.GFSstudio.com

Scripture quotations marked (NIV) are taken from the Holy Bible, New International Version®, NIV®. Copyright © 1973, 1978, 1984, 2011 by Biblica, Inc.™ Used by permission of Zondervan. All rights reserved worldwide. www.zondervan.com The "NIV" and "New International Version" are trademarks registered in the United States Patent and Trademark Office by Biblica, Inc.™

Morgan James is a proud partner of Habitat for Humanity Peninsula and Greater Williamsburg. Partners in building since 2006.

Get involved today! Visit
MorganJamesPublishing.com/giving-back

Table of Contents

Acknowledgements

To my wife, my parents, my brothers, and all of my family—thank you for your unwavering love and support. To all of my friends and colleagues, I am forever grateful for your kindness and encouragement. To the patients I have treated over the years—thank you for the privilege of your trust. I have gained so much from all of you. And last but not least, thank you to my editor and the rest of the team at Morgan James Publishing. This book would not exist without each of you.

Introduction

I have felt the pain of this world. I work with people every day who are depressed, anxious, and fearful. People who lack hope and feel broken and alone. People who face addictions, experience trauma, struggle in relationships, and don't see the value in their lives. The psychological pressures they wrestle with are enormous. Their senses are overwhelmed, and many have chosen to merely exist rather than truly live. We live in an age of frequent distractions and sensory overload. Now more than ever, we need guidance on how to win the battles of our minds.

I, too, have been through seasons of doubt and discouragement. I have dealt with the disappointment of unmet expectations, known the pain of dreams unfulfilled, and felt trapped in a mindset of scarcity. I struggled with the tension of things I could not control. But I survived, and I have a prescription for healing to share with you.

As I was finalizing the initial manuscript for this book, I received notice that one of my former patients committed suicide. She succumbed to the weight of depression and saw death as the only reprieve from her suffering. I was deeply saddened but not surprised. I knew she struggled to find hope in the midst of her pain. And I know there are countless others like her who desperately need a message of hope and connection. I moved with a renewed sense of determination and urgency to complete this book. I pray it helps those in need of a new direction.

Though I am a physician by trade, this book is not a medical text nor a scientific explanation of how the brain works. It is an extension of my divine calling. It is an experience of encouragement and growth. I am here to heighten your awareness of the invisible. I aim to restore your faith, help you live with purpose, and remind you that you are not alone.

I wish you only the fruits of the Spirit: love, joy, peace, patience, kindness, goodness, faithfulness, gentleness, and self-control.

I am deeply grateful that you have chosen to take this journey with me.

Thank you for your trust.

I pray that the secrets of life and God's perfect plans for you are revealed in the pages ahead.

With all my love,

Adam Meadows, MD

Chapter One

Making the Diagnosis

---

*"The wound is the place where the Light
enters you." ~ Jalaluddin Rumi*

FINDING THE LIGHT

We all have disease within us. Dis-ease. An absence of ease. A lack of comfort. We feel unsettled. We experience hardships, inconveniences, and challenges—many of which are self-imposed. These are the conditions and afflictions that cause unrest in our souls.

There are many ways to describe the invisible obstacles that get in the way of our evolution. We use different terms and labels to explain our ailments. For some, it's doubt. For others, it's shame. For many of us, it's fear, anxiety, procrastination, anger, guilt, or regret. We often make the mistake of comparing our disease to others, using assumptions and unfair measurements. We fail to realize that suffering has no judge. We are all subject to the same fate if we don't move in the direction of healing.

In September 2018, I was on a cruise ship in the most beautiful parts of the Mediterranean. The sights were breathtaking. There was a richness to the history, and the flavors, and the culture. But my senses were dulled. I was unhappy. I was in a season of doubt and discouragement. I was not where I wanted to be spiritually, financially, or relationally. I sat in the cabin, silent tears rolling down my cheeks, after my wife and I questioned the state of our marriage and future. I knew I couldn't sustain that level of discontent. I had a deep conviction that we were capable of more. That I could do better. Be more. Give more. I knew I could change and realize the life that my spirit called me to create. That was a personal turning point and a catalyst for this book.

So many people are living in dark seasons right now. Maybe you've lost hope and your faith is fragile. Don't give up. This chapter may not be your best, but your story is not yet finished. This will be a journey of purpose and meaning. We were created with a deep desire to know who we are and why we are here. You have gifts and secrets inside of you waiting to be revealed and understood. I pray the words of this book guide you to revelation. We are in this, doing this work, together.

ASKING THE RIGHT QUESTIONS

Let us begin with an understanding of disease in the clinical context. In my work, I assess complex patterns of symptoms and organize them in order to make a diagnosis. My role involves science, art, and detective work. A diagnosis is simply a shared understanding that allows medical professionals to communicate effectively with patients and with one another. We are trained in a process. We think systematically in protocols and algorithms. We review data from multiple sources and try to construct a narrative that helps make sense of the patient's experience. The ultimate goal of making an accurate diagnosis is to prescribe the right treatment. We aim to cure the disease—or at least improve it. In the same way, making the diagnosis for our mental and emotional limitations is the beginning of our journey toward self-awareness. This requires time, patience, and a commitment to yourself. We must be intentional in getting to know ourselves, spending quality time with ourselves, and being curious about ourselves. We have to ask the right questions, empowering questions: *What am I to learn from this? How can I be of service today? How can I grow through this challenge?* This may also involve consulting with other people who know us well and care about us. We must become students of self, and we must aim to excel.

> **We run the risk of remaining sick the more we try to deny or avoid our reality.**

We cannot change a disease we refuse to acknowledge. Denial keeps the disease locked within. It weakens our immune system and makes us prone to other ailments. That's the unfortunate irony of being sick: When you're already feeling poorly, it's easier to catch something else and feel even worse. Our bodies are more vulnerable in a state of illness. There are certain viral infections that make our bodies more susceptible to bacterial infections, and you acquire what's called a "superinfection." That's literally the phrasing. The premise is that it's hard to fight when we're already weak. The same goes for our emotional health. Once we're already depressed and negative, it's easier to acquire attitudes of resentment, doubt, frustration, apathy, or shame. Like attracts like. Thus, negativity breeds more negativity. And conversely, positivity tends to breed more positive things. That's why it's important that we make active efforts to cultivate our health.

As we're in this process of making a diagnosis for our personal limitations, we need to step back and really look at the patterns in our lives. We have to look for how our diseases manifest over time. And we must be honest with ourselves. We do this by assessing our belief systems, values, behaviors, and thought patterns. It involves the decisions we make, who we surround ourselves with, and what we do with our time. All of these things shed light on our movement toward health or our remaining stuck in illness.

A PRESCRIPTION FOR HEALING

Here are some actionable steps you can take to identify and work through your disease:

Step One: Admit that you have Dis-ease.

This should not come as a surprise. Many of the popular recovery models, such as Alcoholics Anonymous, start with acknowledging that there's a problem. This applies to the diseases of self as well.

Step Two: Understand that your Dis-ease is curable.

We have to adopt a mindset that what we are experiencing is fixable and really believe it. We must remember we are not the first segment of humanity to experience hardships in life. So often our present struggles make us self-absorbed and create tunnel vision against the broader reality that there may be solutions to our problems. There are unlimited stories throughout time about how people have overcome challenges. People with major life crises such as wars, famines, relationship problems, struggles with raising kids, employment issues, spiritual conflicts, and so many others. There are precedents for human suffering. It's therefore prudent for us to investigate the past and acknowledge that people have overcome similar challenges before us.

Step Three: Believe that *you* are deserving of this cure.

This taps into self-worth and self-esteem. We need to believe that we don't have to suffer through whatever is plaguing us. Even if we made choices that got us into this position, we don't deserve to stay there. We are deserving of good things in life. We are deserving of abundance. We are deserving of health, and growth, and progress, and happiness. These are innate human entitlements that God created us with.

Step Four: Commit to the healing process.

We have to resolve to do whatever it takes—face the hard truths, be willing to change, follow sound advice from loved ones, and seek counsel from others who are experts. Commit to do the work of addressing whatever you're suffering from. And as an extension of committing to the healing process, you are committing to investing in your relationship with yourself. Committing to personal reflective time, investigative time, and taking inventory of your life. You'll assess what you're doing, what you're feeling, what you're thinking, and why you're feeling, thinking, and doing those things. And, ultimately, putting energy toward finding solutions. There's an old cliché that says negative people have a

problem for every solution. And I think that there's some truth to that. In contrast, the optimist says there's a solution for every problem. You have to make the shift to solution-focused rather than problem-focused. This is essential for your chances of recovery.

A final thought for these steps toward healing is about your mindset along this journey. Clothe yourself in attitudes of humility, receivership, trust, and vulnerability. When we go to a doctor, we're putting ourselves in the hands of someone else. There's an implicit trust in that relationship, and a transaction takes place. We are going to bring them something—usually problems, disease, symptoms, signs, etc. And they're going to give us something—a prescription, recommendation, a sympathetic ear, comfort, etc. It is this exchange of problems for healing that completes this therapeutic transaction.

Acknowledge the wounds. Let the Light in. Receive the healing. I'm here to speak life into you and remind you that you were made on purpose, with a purpose. You are on a path of restoration. You are more than your Disease. You are worthy of the cure. And You are not alone.

PURPOSE IN PRACTICE

- We all have doubts and go through difficult seasons. Find gratitude and connection to help you endure the dark while reaching for the light.

- The process of growth is uncomfortable. That's why we have *growing pains*. But the results are worth it. I believe in you. And you can do this!
- Healing happens when you shift from a place of criticism to curiosity. Don't judge yourself. Be curious instead. Be a student of yourself and seek to learn and understand.

Chapter Two

Finding the Right Treatment

---

*"The secret of change is to focus all of your
energy, not on fighting the old, but building
the new." ~ Socrates*

TONGUE-TIED

When I was a kid, I had a fairly prominent stutter. I was terribly anxious and self-conscious about it. Even now it brings up uncomfortable memories. There were times in elementary school when the teacher would call on me, and I would pretend I didn't know the answer because I felt the stutter arise in my throat before I could even get the words out. I didn't want to feel humiliated. And what was even worse was having to introduce ourselves in a new classroom at the beginning of a school year. We would go around, one by

9

one, saying our names, where we were from, and a fun fact about ourselves—or some other "icebreaker." But the only ice I felt was in the pit of my stomach. I would fake like I had to use the restroom immediately and scurry out of the classroom before it was my turn. It was awful. And when I had to speak, and inevitably stutter, people were often patient and sympathetic. Some kids snickered, and certain teachers found it endearing. Adults would often say, "It's okay … just take your time" or "Sound it out, honey." The most deflating was when someone would finish the word for me. It sucked, even though I knew they were trying to be helpful.

My parents had me work with a speech therapist. I imagine this helped some. But you want to know what probably helped the most? Speaking. Continuing to do the exact thing that terrified me was the only way to overcome it. I learned that no amount of progress comes from avoidance. We have to do the things that scare us in order to grow and step into our purpose. I still stutter to some extent, but it doesn't consume me the way it used to. I no longer hold back or shrink away from opportunities because of my fear. The truth is that our greatest victories in life will often come through our insecurities.

The journey to living within one's purpose is one of conviction and mindset. We have to constantly reassess and confirm we are on the path to healing. We must choose the right beliefs every day.

> **Any treatment you receive is only as valuable as your willingness to accept it.**

Norman Vincent Peale, one of the fathers of positive thinking, stated, "Medication is of course important; but do not conclude that a pill dissolving in your stomach is necessarily more powerful than a healing thought in your mind." Healing starts with belief. We start with making an accurate diagnosis, meaning acknowledging our diseases, and then move forward to find the right treatment. It's uniquely important in this stage to have a narrow focus.

WISDOM IN SIMPLICITY

Let's say you're working on starting a clothing business. You have all sorts of ideas, have been sketching designs, going to fabric stores, and consuming more Pinterest than should be allowed. And now you've reached a bit of a dead end where you need some outside help. You probably wouldn't register for classes in physical therapy, or purchase a textbook on gardening in South America as your next step. Those things are not in alignment with your goal. You want to start a clothing business; therefore, you want to match the goal with the right educational path or resources.

I know a lot of this sounds intuitive, but it's important to emphasize because sometimes we get distracted and start making decisions that have nothing to do with where we want to go. Or we get "paralysis by analysis" because we're trying to "drink from a fire hose" and consume too many resources at once. We eventually lose focus and become discouraged. We start doing things like starting multiple projects and not finishing them, writing down a bunch of business ideas and not pursuing any of them, or really just getting overwhelmed, lost in the process. There is no reward in this. No progress. This is why staying focused, pursuing goals with intentionality, and approaching treatment with specificity is vital to growth.

We can also learn from people who have come before us. The great Jim Rohn stated, "Success leaves clues. Be a better observer of the winners and the losers, those who are doing well and those who are falling behind. Take mental notes and say: 'I'm going to adjust to what I'm doing based on what I see.'" In other words, you don't need to reinvent the wheel. Let's say you want to work in marketing. You're certainly not the first person in history to want to do this. You're not pioneering a new concept. So, you can start by finding successful marketers to model your journey after.

Let's broaden this and say you are by chance pioneering a new thing. It's likely that there are enough similarities within existing industries that you can piece an initial plan together with some confidence. Maybe you want to be the first person to fly a bicycle across the state of Louisiana. Well, you can read about the mechanics of bicycles, learn the styles of craftsmanship, ride bicycles more often, interview cyclists, etc. You can also read about general aviation principles and how to make objects fly. You can study the weather patterns and air currents in Louisiana, the topography and altitudes, etc. So, even if you're going to be the first person to attempt something, there are often other people who have done parts of what you're seeking to accomplish.

Now, I don't mean to insult your intelligence by being overly simplistic here. This is just one illustration. It gets broader and more complex when we're talking about things like new technologies, for example. Take the advent of the internet. There wasn't really a "pre-internet." Someone saw a problem or an opportunity and had an idea for how to solve it. All of the greatest wonders that we see started as ideas.

Ideas are thoughts with purpose.

Thoughts that people wrestled with, refined, processed, and ultimately put into tangible form through action and persistence.

Don't be shy about following in the footsteps of people who've gone before you. Seek mentorship earnestly. If you can't find someone who's done exactly what you're seeking to do, you can find people who can coach you on the process of pursuing a goal. There are common principles that apply regardless of trade, industry, or end goal. Principles such as: staying motivated, being consistent, and practicing discipline. Those things will help you maintain hope when you're frustrated, move past obstacles, and overcome objections (and rejections). When you think about any high-performing athlete, they still work under the training of a coach, even though they're very talented. They know there is value in an outside perspective and the accountability that comes with it. Even if your coach doesn't have the same talent you have, they can often see things you can't. They can advise in areas where they see room for improvement. Thus, mentorship, supervision, or coaching of some sort is a key ingredient for success. This will accelerate your progress toward learning something new, having more of something desirable, or ridding yourself of something undesirable.

You must maintain narrow focus here too. You want to look in the right places for that support. For example, if you are looking to do something that involves a certain amount of risk, you may want to look for a coach or mentor who's taken risk before. If you want to pursue something that's particularly scarce or highly competitive, you may want a coach who's well-connected or has influence. So, even if the specific thing that you're pursuing is different from what your coach has accomplished, there should be enough overlapping themes, and you look for your mentors in those places of overlap.

FINDING BALANCE

As you can see, all of these themes are connected. We have to make an accurate diagnosis and then piece together the right treatment plan to achieve our goals. This journey is about progress, not perfection. The purpose is to be thoughtful in your approach and to develop a plan that involves taking action with support along the way. There are going to be roadblocks, hiccups, and side effects (which we'll explore in a later chapter). There will be times when you don't want to take your proverbial "medication"—times when you are sick of it or don't think you need any more. All of the usual things that get in the way of progress in clinical medicine also occur in our life journeys toward personal development and success.

Allow me to end with a word of caution about overdose. Earlier we covered the pitfall of trying to consume too many resources at once: "drinking from a fire hose." This can also be conceptualized as overdosing, an inherent risk of the process of pursuing our purpose. Sometimes harm can come from too much of a good thing. We are at risk of burning out if we stay only in ambition and "Go, Go, Go" mode too long.

This is often reinforced by societal norms these days. There is a lot of glamour associated with "the grind" and "the hustle" and gluttonous hashtags like "#Team-NoSleep." While these may seem inspirational, they are missing the mark and setting people up for running out of gas. It's okay to work hard, but we have to be cautious not to work to excess. We need to balance our drive with adequate rest. We are more likely to create sustainable success when we pace ourselves and listen to our bodies rather than allowing our fatigue to stifle motivation.

For some, a solution might be working smarter, not harder, i.e., balance and efficiency. We have to be mindful not to overwork to the point of crippling ourselves, wherein we wouldn't be able to enjoy the rewards of what we've worked so hard to attain. Perhaps you've lost friends or family members or burned bridges because you were too focused on achievement. You neglected what truly matters in life because you "overdosed" on your goals. If so, it's time to reset your priorities and take care of your most important asset along the way: yourself. You are the vehicle of your success. Make time for rest stops and oil changes. Check and recalibrate the GPS, rotate your tires, and get a car wash. Take a moment to park at the top of a scenic highway and enjoy the view. For this is your journey, and you are in the driver's seat. Ignore the traffic. There is no rush. Arriving at your purpose is worth the wait. And You are not alone.

PURPOSE IN PRACTICE

- The key to success lies in the alignment of our true inner being (i.e., who we are) with how we operate in the world.
- Not only is it okay to ask for help—it's necessary. None of us is meant to go through this journey alone.
- Take care of yourself. And be kind to your body. You are in a monogamous, inseparable relationship with yourself for the rest of your life. You might as well enjoy it!

Chapter Three

The Placebo Effect

_"All of us are connected to this limitless power
and most of us aren't using but a fraction of it."_
~ Jen Sincero

YOU GET WHAT YOU EXPECT

From a young age, doing things with excellence was instilled in me. My parents encouraged me to always do my best, and they modeled this in their lives. They kept their commitments. They were faithful and ambitious in their careers. I don't think I saw my father miss a day of work for the 18 years I was living at home. He was the epitome of consistency.

My desire for excellence was particularly apparent in my academic work. I valued making good grades. It was a symbol of achievement and esteem. I remember the sense of disappointment I felt when I was a few points shy of testing into the "target" program (i.e., gifted classes) in middle school. My closest friends were in that program, and I believed I belonged there, too. I carried this mindset with me to college. I made straight As my freshman year and ultimately graduated summa cum laude—with *highest* honors. I don't say this to brag; I say this to show what is possible. What started as an external expectation set *for* me became an *internalized* belief. I believed I was capable of academic excellence. As I saw the results, my confidence grew, and I continued to perform at a high level.

Mel Robbins, author of *The 5 Second Rule*, talks about confidence in a profound way. She talks about it not as a personality trait or something that we are born with but as a skill that can be developed with practice. It is malleable and situational, and it does not depend on feelings. You can have high confidence in some areas and low confidence in others. My academic confidence grew as a result of the decisions I made and the effort I put into my schoolwork. I engaged in behaviors that were in line with my desired outcome. This is the crux of the placebo effect: the power of belief and the actions you take as a result. In this chapter, I invite you to examine your values and beliefs. What principles do you hold tightly in your core? Who put them there? Do you still believe them? Once you have clarity on these questions, aim to live each day in alignment with the values that bring cohesion and meaning to your life. This shows up as you starting to place more of your time, energy, and resources in the things that truly matter to you. The decisions you make and the people you spend time with are a reflection of what you value. And when that is not the case, you have a clearer sense of how things got off track.

In the medical sense, the placebo effect occurs as a byproduct of trying to prove the efficacy of an unknown treatment. Let's use a research study on antidepressant medications as an example. One group of patients is taking an active form of medication, and the other group is taking a sugar pill (i.e., a placebo). What researchers have found, in the best case, is the placebo response is upward of 30 to 40 percent. Meaning, 30 to 40 percent of people taking an inactive form of medication are experiencing similar benefits and relief as those taking the active form. This phenomenon is fascinating from a psychological perspective and underscores the power of belief.

> **Our belief in something influences our experience of the outcome.**

As scientists have dissected the placebo effect more carefully, what they've seen is that the other aspects of a relationship with a medical professional make a substantial difference. So, in the case of an antidepressant study, the patients who were taking the placebo are also engaging in behaviors that are likely to make them feel better. They are meeting with the doctor regularly, feeling cared for, and having conversations in which they feel heard. At each visit, the patients taking the placebo are getting up, getting dressed, leaving the house, and going to a medical office or treatment center—an identical process as the patients taking an active form of medication. The process influences belief, which influences the outcome. This same phenomenon applies to our personal improvement journeys as well. We must start from a place of strong belief. We must feel a conviction that what we're doing is meaningful, impactful, and beneficial.

CULTIVATING THE RIGHT MINDSET

Here are a few actions that support and reinforce your desired beliefs:

- Write daily "I Am" statements that affirm your personal growth.
  - I am moving toward my goals with purpose and clarity.
  - I am capable of achieving exactly what I want.
  - I am attracting success and opportunity into my life.
- Consume positive content every day.

- Read inspirational stories of people pursuing similar goals.
- Watch uplifting videos.
- Listen to music that makes you feel energized and hopeful.
- Measure your progress with self-compassion and patience.
  - Focus on what you've accomplished rather than what's missing.
  - Block time for rest and "play" in your schedule proactively.
  - Celebrate each milestone of progress along the way.

Engaging in these practices with intention and consistency is certain to increase your chances of success. Imagine someone who is training to be a long-distance runner. They have an end goal of running a marathon. As they train, they are focusing on improving their pace and building stamina. They work on their mindset to ignore the fatigue and pain in their legs. There are going to be some days when they don't feel like running. The weather may be nasty outside, they didn't sleep well the night before, they're feeling sore, there's a schedule conflict—any number of reasons. And they are feeling torn between sticking with the process of training or giving in to their feelings or excuses. If they want to be prepared for the marathon, they must choose to keep going. In the same way, you must choose to keep going. You have to appreciate the importance of continuing the behaviors you know will prepare you for your goal. Going through the motions matters. I use these same strategies in my own development journey. It's not always easy, but it's worth it. Even when we're not at our goal yet, we maintain a strong belief that we're on track, and our behaviors will be in accordance with this belief.

In a misunderstood sense, we have this social cliché of "fake it till you make it." The term has a dismissive and somewhat insincere connotation. The principle suggests that we go through the motions, put a smile on our face, and pretend we are someone we are not. That tone has always rubbed me the wrong way. There's an implied lack of authenticity that I don't believe is accurate. We're not actually *faking* anything.

> **We are practicing the things we aspire to become.**

When a child is learning to ride a bike and falls down, we don't respond by saying, "You're not a bike rider. Stop pretending!" We recognize that they are practicing. They are going through the motions of learning to ride a bike more skillfully—just like with our efforts toward personal growth. We are making decisions and being intentional about what we're thinking, saying, and doing in the service of who we are becoming. We are building our muscles of purpose. And there is nothing fake or inauthentic about that.

Separating our feelings from our behaviors is critical for our success and achievement. We have to choose to engage in effective behaviors regardless of how we feel and, oftentimes, in opposition to how we feel. There are going to be days when we don't feel like getting up and going to work. Or days when we don't feel like exercising. Or dealing with our spouses. Or driving past the fast-food restaurant. Or writing this book chapter. This is called being human. Yet, in spite of our feelings, we have to make decisions that we know are in the service of what we're ultimately trying to achieve. We should embrace consistency, value progress, and trust the process of growth. And it all starts with cultivating a strong belief in what we're doing and the conviction that we're worth doing it for.

PRACTICE MAKES PROGRESS

This brings me to another theme worth noting. There is a difference between *feeling* better and *getting* better. Many therapists reference this contrast in their work with patients. Feeling better is an inner sensation that gives us tangible evidence that we are healing. We stop crying. Our sleep improves. Our cough goes away. Getting better is a more subtle experience. It requires repeated effort over time and is something we appreciate in hindsight rather than along the way.

Can you remember learning an instrument when you were younger? I imagine it didn't feel so great as you were doing it, particularly in the early stages. You couldn't read the music, you hit the wrong notes, and you had very little interest in practicing. But for those of you who stuck with it (myself not included), pushed past your doubts, and corrected your errors, you ultimately got better. You developed a sense of proficiency and the amount of effort you had to exert gradually diminished. It may have taken six months or six years, but you made it. So instead of analyzing each individual experience, good or bad, we have to look at the trajectory of where we started versus where we are going. We have to value a better finish line more than a better feeling along the way. And trust that with each step, successful or not, we are getting closer to our goals.

The placebo effect—the power of belief—is a very real and valuable phenomenon. It is an asset, not an accident. When we reflect on the placebo effect in medical literature, we see it has a powerful impact. The same goes for our personal journeys. Making decisions and taking steps that are positive and purposeful, independent of how we feel, is paramount to our success. This is a divine reminder that our success doesn't lie in the tools we use. It does not lie in the money, the gym membership, the new job, the fancy guitar, the seminars we attend, or even the experts who advise us. The keys to success lie within.

Success is intimately tied to your belief that growth and advancement are in your DNA. I am here to affirm that you were designed intelligently and specifically. There were no errors or accidents in your formation. Your Creator did not leave anything up to chance. There is an inner wisdom guiding you to your divine calling. Listen to it. Believe it. Move on it. For you are tremendously special. You are one of a kind. And You are not alone.

PURPOSE IN PRACTICE

- Whatever you do, do it with excellence. The levels of energy and intention that you apply to the process affect the outcome.
- Learn to value the process of *becoming* over the desired goal.
- Our beliefs shape our reality. Take time to explore what you believe, why you believe it, and how that belief adds value to your life.

A NEW RESOLUTION

Some of you are discouraged.

You've had enough of this year, and you can't wait for the new year to come.

You've lost some friends, gained some problems, and experienced some hardships this year that you'd prefer to forget.

You've thought, "If only I had more time ... more money ... a better marriage ... more support at work ... better health ... fewer obstacles. If only ... things would have been different this year."

You're convinced that a turn of the calendar will bring about a new season in your life.

Friends, what if I told you there is a higher purpose for everything you've been through?

What if I told you the situation you're in now is exactly where you're supposed to be?

I'm here to remind you that your current reality is part of your divine assignment.

And it's time to change your "If Only" to "I Am."
I am worthy.
I am capable.
I am deserving of goodness.
I am called for a special purpose.
I am growing in clarity each day.
I am not alone.
You have the ability to experience all that is good simply by shifting your attention, and asking The Giver to provide.
You don't have to wait until next year to be free from your pain.
Your deliverance is now.
Step into it!
And take confidence that the resolutions you seek have already been prepared for your benefit.

Chapter Four

Side Effects

---

*"Although the world is full of suffering, it is also
full of the overcoming of it."* ~ *Helen Keller*

THE PRISON OF NONCOMMITMENT

The social side of what undergrad was for most
people was what medical school was like for
me. Sure, I had some fun in college, but I was
laser focused on academics and went to a fairly strict
institution. We had gender-specific dorms and curfew all
four years. It snowed six months out of the year, and the
nearest "big city" was South Bend, Indiana. Take that for
what it's worth. So, medical school was a bit of an awak-
ening for my independence and freedom. I lived on my
own for the first time. I developed a core group of male
friends with whom I'm still in regular contact today. We

have a group chat that's full of high school boy humor, birthday shout-outs, and "this is the year" promises of resuming our annual guys' trip. Back then we took our studies seriously but also made it a priority to have fun, and I have lots of good memories from those early mornings and late nights! However, one thing I promised myself was that I was not going to enter a serious relationship too early.

Prior to med school, I was a serial over-committer, and it took a toll on me emotionally. I was tired. I was jaded. And, most importantly, I was afraid of getting hurt. I wanted to maintain the upper hand at all times. I didn't want any serious relationship commitments or encumbrances, as I knew the rigors of medical school would be challenging enough on their own. So I "dated around" those first three years. I didn't have a plan, didn't really have criteria on what I was looking for or what I should avoid. What started as a journey in relationship freedom left me confused with unbalanced attachments. I had a script of repeated explanations of why I needed to pull away when things were feeling too serious. These were the side effects of running away from monogamy. It didn't feel good. I became lost in the process of pursuing without committing, and it was an emotional merry-go-round. I was unfulfilled. After a couple years, I knew I needed an exit strategy. By the grace of God, I made it out with minimal scarring and enough clarity to secure a relationship with the woman who would later become my wife.

All that to say side effects are a natural part of our personal development journeys. These are the "life happens" moments, unexpected events, and the bad that comes along with the good. Which raises the question: How do we manage this? How do we deal with the unintended consequences of our decisions?

Well, it starts with acceptance.

> **We must grow to accept setbacks, mistakes, and failure as a necessary part of the process.**

Side effects are inevitable. They will occur from within just as much as from the external world. Our minds will produce fear, doubt, judgment, shame, and a myriad of other pitfalls if we allow it to drift too far. We must cultivate a discipline of centering our thoughts daily. In the medical sense, we consider side effects to be the undesirable effects of a medication.

So, if we're taking medicine to help lower our blood pressure, some of the potential side effects we might experience include numbness, tingling, blurry vision, or headaches. The same mechanisms by which it lowers our blood pressure lead to these other physical effects. This represents the larger principle that anything we put into our body or do to our body affects our whole system. As a healthcare community, we've labeled side effects as something bad, but they really are an inherent part of the medication's activity. Side effects are evidence that the medication is working. Thus, we artificially distinguish symptom relief as the pleasant effect of medication and side effects as the unpleasant effect. But, in reality, they are one and the same.

GETTING A NEW WARDROBE

Along the path to success, there are going to be side effects. There are choices we make, experiences we have, or things that happen to us that feel unpleasant. But it's important to accept those things as part of the process. Instead of avoiding or stigmatizing our mistakes, we need to shift our mindset and start embracing those things as necessary parts of the journey. In fact, expecting or welcoming those things can be very helpful to reframe the paradigm of what this process involves. We need to lean into hardships and difficult experiences that are in the service of our growth. It's how we develop resilience to press forward.

Let's take a closer look at the "how" behind managing a side effect. We'll go back to our weight loss example and unpack the experience of low motivation or discouragement. In the process of losing weight, we embark on a plan of changing our behaviors around food and exercise. We try to eat fewer calories, limit unhealthy foods, drink more water, and exercise regularly. As a bonus, we also try to get adequate sleep and place ourselves in environments that are going to help keep us on track. We may join Weight Watchers, attend an exercise class, or participate in a support group. These are things we all can identify as the expected parts of the weight loss process.

Now, let's look at one of the side effects: buying new clothes. Your larger clothes no longer fit once you've lost considerable weight. You have to go to the store (or online) and purchase new clothing. You may be required to spend money you didn't originally budget for. Is this a hardship? Possibly. But would the average person choose not to lose weight because of the inconvenience of having to purchase new clothing? No! In fact, most people might actually embrace that as a good thing. But there's a cost, a literal financial cost, in having to purchase a new wardrobe to accommodate a smaller size. This can either be a side effect or a desired outcome—it all depends on your perspective.

Choosing the right perspective and beliefs about your success journey is so critical. Disapproval from family can be a side effect—or an opportunity to expand your support system to others outside of your family. Rejection from friends can be a side effect—or an opportunity to build your relationship with yourself and with God. Not getting a promotion at work can be a side effect—or an opportunity to finally take that leap of faith into entre-preneurship. It's all in your perspective.

| **Learn to see your losses as opportunities.**

TIME IS FERTILIZER

One thing to keep in mind is that most side effects are temporary. When you start a new medication, you may have an upset stomach or a headache. But in most cases, it won't be for the lifetime of the medication. It's a temporary side effect. Your body will eventually acclimate and learn to interpret these side effects as harmless, and you might not even notice whatever it was after a few weeks.

The same goes for the discomfort of growth. They are called "growing pains" for a reason. Stay the course, and you will get to the other side. Don't abandon the journey just because the early phase is uncomfortable. Your spiritual growth is like exercise. It may be unpleas-ant in the beginning, but, in a short while, you build enough strength and endurance to keep going. And you notice that the process becomes a little easier and a little more natural along the way. You may even start to look forward to "working out"—literally and metaphorically.

Oftentimes, we experience the side effects of change before the benefits. It requires us to practice a mindset of long-term gain over short-term inconvenience in order to stay the course. For example, let's say you have a broken leg. You're in pain and can't walk. You go to the emergency room and consult with a surgeon. She shows you the X-rays to point out the injury and confirms you need surgery. She then explains all the intricacies of the procedure. She describes where she'll have to cut your leg open, realign your bones, and insert screws and a metal plate. It sounds like a tutorial at Home Depot. Your face cringes at the prospect of the carpentry work your body is about to endure. It doesn't sound pleasant at all. In fact, parts of the surgery and recovery may be worse than your current pain. But you choose to go through with the surgery because you trust that healing lies on the other side of the pain.

In the same way, happiness lies on the other side of our depression. Protection lies on the other side of our abuse. Love lies on the other side of our loneliness. The Universe is quietly conspiring for our good at all times. You are more than the side effects that beset you. You are getting closer to your divine purpose with each step. You can finish this race. And You are not alone.

PURPOSE IN PRACTICE

- Unfocused efforts lead to poor results. Be decisive and focused about what you pursue. It's okay to change your mind along the way, but start with clarity as you take the first step.

- Success is not a linear path. It is a marathon, not a sprint. Learn to play the long game and anticipate challenges along the way.
- You must practice accepting the bad along with the good. You have no chance of getting through life without pain or difficulty of some sort. Learn your tolerances, and learn to heal quickly.
- Learn to see opportunities rather than limitations.

Chapter Five

Noncompliance

"The greatest glory in living lies not in never falling, but in rising every time we fall." ~ Nelson Mandela

HABIT BEATS MOTIVATION

More often than not, we get in the way of our own success. We drift. We get distracted. We take breaks longer than planned, and we lose momentum. It's usually unintentional. But there are also times when our sabotage is more deliberate. We lose interest and get a case of "I don't feel motivated anymore." We rely on things like feelings and motivation to keep us on track.

I've learned that relying on feelings is likely to end in failure or disappointment. Motivation is as reliable as quicksand. It begins to fade as soon as it comes. Not to say that seeking motivation or inspiration is worthless. Both have value, but they also have their limitations. They are not the building blocks of sustained progress.

We have to create the habits for success.

A habit is a behavior we engage in with little to no conscious thought. Most of us have habits of brushing our teeth, getting dressed, or heading to Starbucks for our morning coffee as we prepare for the workday. There are also habits we develop out of boredom or avoidance, such as mindlessly scrolling on social media. And then we have emotional habits such as worrying, complaining, gossiping, and blaming. These are all things we do automatically and things that can begin to erode our character if we are not mindful about correcting them.

Our habits are either in service of our growth, or they are keeping us stagnant. We must be intentional about developing habits with purpose. Let's say we want to start a business. Some of the habits in service of this would include writing down our ideas, reading books and articles about business, and attending networking events or seminars. We may also invest time in researching the industry, learning about our customers, knowing our competitors, and identifying sources of funding. These are habits and behaviors that help get our business off the ground and increase the likelihood of success. It's important to develop and commit to these habits early in the process. Motivation and the pace of opportunity will wax and wane. We only have control over our efforts and decisions—and the habits that influence them.

In the journey toward purpose, noncompliance can also take the shape of overconfidence. We fall into the trap of thinking we know better than the experts and those who have charged this path ahead of us. There is a difference between healthy confidence and arrogance. In my profession, one of my biggest tongue-in-cheek competitors is "Dr. Google." We have access to all kinds of information on the internet, and not all of it is medically sound. We can scour the web for what symptoms could mean, and it can be a rabbit hole without the proper knowledge or training. There are patient testimonials with lots of hyperbole, alarmist websites designed to draw distrust of pharmaceutical companies, and other unfounded information. You type in headache and stomach pain, and next thing you know, you have Stage 4 liver cancer! This is both exaggerated and risky. Taking symptoms out of context is likely to result in misdiagnosis, and, worse, improper treatment. As physicians, discernment is a skill we cultivate through knowledge and experience.

I'm not here to suggest that the internet is a dangerous place altogether. There is good medical information on the internet, and physicians rely on it every day as well. We consult with one another on physician groups and forums, review research articles on PubMed, and use apps on our smartphones to double-check for issues with diagnosis or medication interactions. But these are tools we use only after we've completed the requisite training. Putting a teenager behind the wheel of car before they have an understanding of the vehicle can be dangerous. Similarly, putting yourself in the position of both patient and physician can be risky. We have to exercise caution against pride and over-confidence and the I-can-figure-this-out-on-my-own complex.

YOU DON'T KNOW A BETTER WAY

We also run the risk of creating things from scratch unnecessarily. One of the greatest time-wasters is not following directions—directions often created by some-one who already knows the fastest (or safest) way to pro-ceed. The great Jim Rohn stated: "Success leaves clues."

But, of course, we think our story is different. We say, "Their path doesn't apply to me" or "I think I have a better way." And while that may be true, it's unproven. There are times when you may need to blaze a new trail, but don't neglect the multitude of well-established trails along the way. I wasn't the first physician to go to med-ical school, nor did I waste time pursuing a path outside of medical school to try to become a physician. Medical school was the way. It's important to have enough humility to accept that there are some things we can learn from other people who've been there before us. And we need to have enough discipline and patience to follow the course. We fall into unnecessary detours when we expect quick fixes, take shortcuts, or assume we know a better way.

We also have to avoid the dreaded "shiny object" syndrome. Too often, we get distracted by the next best thing if it seems easier, faster, or more lucrative. I can't tell you how many times I've been suckered by this. I've chased a number of opportunities (read: detours) that over-promised and under-delivered on their value.

And it was my own fault.

I didn't listen to the inner wisdom that was encouraging me to stay put and be patient. We must be realistic and accept that no matter which path we take, it's going to take time and consistent effort.

In a spiritual sense, we have to develop and maintain a mindset of surrender to our Higher Power. I call this God. You may choose a different word. The title is less important than the meaning. Our relationship with our Higher Power is the foundation of learning trust. Our divine intuition is always guiding us. Take comfort in that. You don't have to have all the answers. There is The Great Physician, and He is in control. He knows what we need mentally, physically, spiritually, emotionally, financially, and relationally. Moreover, having a spirit that is willing and open to receiving the wisdom of God will illuminate your path. Our greatest error is relying on self instead of trusting our Higher Power. Not only will self-reliance lead to discouragement and frustration, but it also runs the risk of causing us to lose hope and abandon the journey altogether.

THE RISK OF CRUISE CONTROL

In the medical world, noncompliance tends to occur when people start feeling better and think they no longer need treatment. They have thoughts like, "I'm feeling better. Maybe I don't need this medicine anymore" or "Maybe I don't need to go back to physical therapy; maybe I can skip that next visit to the dentist … " etc.

> *Maybe* **is a dangerous word in the journey of living with purpose.**

Certainly, most doctors want you to get better and reach a point where you don't need to follow up as frequently, or, perhaps, at all. However, that discussion has to come in the context of a relationship, a mutual agreement that enough progress has been made to move on. Too often, these decisions are made outside of the office and are unilateral. We allow the experience of feeling better to distort our memory of what it was like being ill.

And we begin to veer off course from the very path (and treatment) that led to our wellness.

We're guilty of noncompliance with our success journey as well. It's kind of like learning to drive. At first, we're extra cautious. We adjust the mirrors, check the tires, keep the gas tank full, and fasten our seatbelt as soon as we get in the car. We're very patient at intersections and make our best effort to stay within the speed limit. Over time, we become more comfortable with the process and start to relax. We don't check the tires as often, and speed limits become more relative. We also learn about features like "cruise control" and, next thing we know, our foot is off the gas. We go on autopilot. We allow our comfort and familiarity to lower our effort and attention.

Yet, we must remember there are other drivers on the road. And the path we're on won't stay straight indefinitely. There will be times when we'll need to slow down, merge into another lane, or get off at an exit. There will be traffic jams and hazardous road conditions. The weather will change, or we may be stuck driving late at night. We cannot allow our confidence behind the wheel to result in passive management of the vehicle.

Too many of us are operating on "cruise control" at the wrong times. We let up on effort and discipline and end up getting into trouble. We cause accidents, literally and metaphorically. We run into people, neglect those we love, and stop treating our bodies and minds with the care they deserve.

> **Purposeful growth requires active management at all times.**

There are also times when we are disloyal to those from whom we are seeking help. Imagine you have a bad cough for several weeks. You tried most over-the-counter remedies with minimal success. You go to the doctor and he confirms you have a mild case of pneumonia. You're a bit surprised, but you trust your doctor and agree to take the prescription he offers you. A couple days go by and you still haven't started the medication. The cough is still there, and you decide to call a friend for a second opinion. They're not sure what to do, but out of support, they align with your skepticism and tell you to "look it up online." Next thing you know, you're in the bowels of a Google search, trying to make sense of the one billion results for the prompt "cough that won't go away." And now you're afraid you may have tuberculosis. You spend the next several hours fraught with anxiety and barely sleep that night. You call the doctor's office the next morning. He answers your questions and calmly explains his certainty that this is pneumonia—and not tuberculosis. You start the medication and begin feeling better in just a few days.

Such is the experience when we deviate from the Source of our help. We waste time in angst and uncertainty rather than trusting the plan that has been laid out for us. It's okay to have questions and even doubts. But give your Provider, your Higher Power, the first opportunity to answer your questions and address your concerns. It is a sacred relationship. And you have a direct connection to Him at all times. Don't make this journey harder than it needs to be. Invite your Higher Power to be your Great Physician. His waiting room is peaceful. He will see you promptly. He always knows what prescription to give you, and His healing is guaranteed. You are His favorite patient. And You are not alone.

PURPOSE IN PRACTICE

- Learn to value habits over feelings. There are things you will need to do that you won't feel like doing in the moment in order to reach your full potential.

- Your uniqueness does not require you to create things from scratch every time. It's okay to follow a well-worn path. Your experience of the journey will be unique in its own way.

- Be intentional with your times of rest. It's okay to slow down and relax sometimes—but don't get complacent or make assumptions about how things are going to proceed. Keep your eyes open and hands on the wheel at all times, and be purposeful when deciding between pressing the gas or the brakes.

Chapter Six

Going Through Withdrawal

"In the end, we only regret the chances we didn't take, relationships we were afraid to have, and the decisions we waited too long to make."
~ Lewis Carroll

THE PROCESS OF EVOLUTION

She did exactly as she was instructed. She listened to her parents and followed the wisdom of tradition. She went to college, got a degree and then went to graduate school and obtained a doctorate. She did the right thing. The safe thing. She sought security in a world that was ever-changing and unpredictable. She pursued higher education with the intent of finding a stable career. After all, she didn't have her parents to guide her anymore. There was no safety net.

So she did as she was told and hoped that reality would go as planned.

Until it didn't.

She entered a career that was not aligned with her calling. There was no passion, drive, or fulfillment in the stability of a 9-to-5 schedule that wasn't meant for her. She settled—and felt unsettled.

And her decision to marry a man who was the captain of playing it safe only magnified her dilemma. Her husband had very traditional expectations and also followed a linear path in his education and career. And he expected the same from her because that's all he knew. He was a physician, and he was content. He sold her on the dream of living comfortably and building a two-income household of working professionals with doctoral degrees. Success was measured in money—a paycheck that you received every two weeks from an employer.

In his vision, they would share the same last name, start a family, live in nice neighborhoods, take some vacations, and retire after paying their dues for many years. They would focus on priorities like paying down debt and saving as much as they could. They wouldn't take too many risks. They knew better. They didn't want to squander what they worked hard to earn. But the problem was that it was *his* dream and *his* plan. The more the husband pressed, the more his wife felt edged out. She felt consumed. Voiceless. Invisible. He became more confused and frustrated. He couldn't understand why she wouldn't want this dream—his dream. And a distance grew between them. They still loved each other but felt helpless in the midst of this inequity.

The woman was going through withdrawal. She was an artist at heart. She was creative, musically inclined, thought in abstract ways, and experienced the world in high definition. Colors were more vibrant, sounds were crisper, and energy more palpable. She lived in a world of the invisible and felt trapped by the tangible. In the face of society's judgment and her husband's narrow views, she began to listen to her heart. There was something deep inside, an inner wisdom, calling her to something more. She knew that staying on the path she was on would lead to ruin—ruin of self, of her marriage, and of the possibility of true happiness. No one would gain from her staying the course and playing it safe.

So, she began to explore and listen to her creative intuitions. She had been writing songs since she was eight years old. Now as an adult, she brought out her guitar and writing pad, and she let her spirit do the rest. She began to create and grow. And then she got the idea to write children's books in honor of her parents' memories.

You see, her parents died together tragically in a car accident when she was only 13 years old. She and her twin sister were in the car with them. They and their driver survived, but their parents didn't. There was no goodbye.

No parting words of comfort or wisdom. The pain of unresolved grief haunted them. She learned at an early age that life was short and could be gone in an instant. Tomorrow was not guaranteed; therefore, there was no purpose in living if she wasn't living with purpose. Slowly but surely, art began to manifest through her. She printed her books, wrote her songs, and grew her footprint on social media. She began to perform in small circles, network, pitch ideas, and take risks. It wasn't glamorous. She struggled and ran into obstacles frequently. Some things didn't materialize, and she got discouraged.

But she never quit.

Her husband went through phases of support and disapproval, praise and criticism. She endured it all and never quit—on her dreams or on their marriage. Now she has produced a number of songs, toured internationally as an opening act for renowned artists, supported orphans through philanthropic efforts, and given lectures at universities on branding and entrepreneurship. She has started a movement and attracted the right people along the way. All because she chose to turn from human expectations and answer her divine calling.

This story is about my wife, with whom I am deeply in love.

I have learned more in my marriage than in all of my years of formal education. My wife inspires me daily, and she was a major catalyst for this book. I am called to write in the same way she is called to create. My traditions kept me safe, but they also kept me in withdrawal. And I didn't realize it until my diseases showed up in my marriage: fear, anxiety, envy, anger, insignificance, the need to control. It was like a mirror. All the flaws that I projected on my wife were representative of illness inside of me. And I was desperately in need of healing.

So, I chose to focus on myself and pursue the things that God was prompting me to do. The more I stepped back, the more He stepped in. I prayed, listened, and practiced obedience. I realized the problems—and the solutions—were all within. They always were. And I came to understand that God is more generous and more merciful than I ever imagined. I have more clarity and peace now than ever before. My wife and I experience greater levels of connection each day. Things are not perfect between us. We accept that they never will be. But we seek God collectively, and individually, and trust that He will continue to fill in the gaps. The pain of withdrawal is gone, and His love supplies all that we need.

LEARN TO LISTEN FROM WITHIN

There will be experiences of withdrawal in this journey. You will need to detox from habits and beliefs that no longer serve you.

It won't be pleasant.

> **You will shed old ways of thinking and engaging as you evolve into a new person.**

I hope this chapter prepares you for that process. Withdrawal can feel like grief because that's what it is. But rest assured that the pain is only temporary—as long as you make the right choices about how you move forward.

If you choose to abandon your divine calling, the suffering and the cravings will persist. There is no way to soften this message. I want this to feel as real as possible.

Let's begin with discussing what withdrawal is in the medical context. There are things that our bodies depend on for survival. We depend on oxygen to breathe. We need our hearts to pump blood to provide nourishment to our organs. Our brains require glucose to function normally. An absence of any of these things will lead to dysfunction in the body, organ failure, and ultimately death. We can also experience withdrawal on a smaller scale with medications. When you abruptly stop a medication, there's a steep decline in the blood levels of that chemical, and your cells signal the alarm bells. It's as if they're saying, "Whoa! Wait a minute. Something is missing here!" Your body goes haywire in the service of prompting you to replace what's missing.

The type of withdrawal you experience depends on the nature of the substance that was taken away. Take alcohol, for instance. Alcohol is naturally a depressant to the central nervous system. This means it can lead to slower breathing, reduced heart rate, sedation, slowness in thinking and coordination, and so on. And, of course, each person has a different tolerance for the amount of alcohol that is required to create these effects. Once someone has been drinking regularly for a while (i.e., months or years), their body develops a physical dependence on it. And when alcohol is abruptly removed from the picture, the withdrawal looks like an excitatory state. They will experience rapid heart rate, sweating, trembling, rapid breathing, confusion, agitation, and elevated blood pressure. Alcohol withdrawal is potentially dangerous and, in the worst-case scenario, can lead to a seizure.

On the other hand, cigarettes provide a contrasting, and less threatening, withdrawal syndrome. When you quit smoking "cold turkey," you can experience headaches, irritability, sleeplessness, and increased appetite. You also crave nicotine, which is the brain's way of signaling that you are missing something and need it back.

These two substances, alcohol and nicotine, illustrate what happens physically and emotionally when we go through withdrawal. It is the result of a physiologic process. And there are parallels for this along our journeys toward self-improvement and living with purpose.

When we abandon our divine calling, we enter a state of withdrawal.

Our spirit tells us that something is missing. We become restless and unfulfilled. We may be able to ignore these feelings for a time. But the withdrawal will keep nagging at us. We can try to find substitutes or distractions, but nothing will satiate our need like the divine substance that is missing.

If you're like me, you sometimes get hung up on reasons to justify why you're not making progress. Or why you quit. Maybe you couldn't secure funding to launch that startup. Or maybe you didn't get the emotional support from loved ones that you were hoping for. Or maybe an unexpected life situation occurs: a relationship begins or ends, a new job, a move, an illness. You can allow any number of things to lead to distraction or discouragement.

You stop pursuing your true purpose.

When you do that, when you ignore your purpose, you're going to experience a sense of loss. Grief will take over and open the door for withdrawal. You will feel a decline in your health somewhere—physically, emotionally, spiritually, or relationally. I know you can relate to this. For some of you, it may have been weeks ago, months ago, or years ago when you veered off track and stopped actively pursuing your purpose. You may have settled for a job, sought security in a relationship, or simply thought you couldn't afford the risk of greatness. You needed something more stable, more predictable.

But that craving for more never left you.

That nagging voice inside your mind keeps whispering, reminding you of what you left—and what you need to return to.

For others, it's a sinking feeling in your stomach or a heaviness in your chest. Your body is telling you what it needs. Don't ignore it. If you're honest with yourself, you know there is a void. You are in withdrawal, which has multiple phases. There is an initial phase where those emotions are really raw and intense. You may be anxious, indecisive, pacing the room, going through old notebooks then putting them down. You're wrestling with yourself. It's like tug of war in your mind. You can step away, and the intensity will die down for a while, but the discomfort never leaves completely. There may be a delayed withdrawal. It's a subtle, protracted phase. It will feel quiet for a time, and then you'll see something on TV or listen in on a conversation that reminds you of that idea you were pursuing. And it triggers the withdrawal experience all over again. You start to fantasize with nostalgia over unfinished dreams, and the cravings for growth and change intensify. You realize your life hasn't been the same since you turned away from your purpose.

SHEDDING OLD LAYERS

Withdrawal is also experienced in the process of pursuing your calling. The experience of getting rid of old habits and limiting beliefs has a sense of withdrawal, too. It can feel just as unpleasant. You probably know people who are in bad relationships or dealing with toxic work environments, and they eventually end the relationship or leave the job. You think to yourself, "Woohoo! Finally! They are free and ready to move on. I'm so glad I don't have to listen to their drama anymore!"

Perhaps you're one of those people, and your friends are saying this about you. It's not so easy being on the other side of a good decision. Even leaving things that are unhealthy can be a struggle. You have mixed feelings. You might miss some things about it, or even start to romanticize the good parts. This is common. But you still get to do the work of letting go. Letting go of procrastination, blame, self-doubt, and fear. There is an emotional and physical shedding of that former self that may leave you feeling naked and vulnerable.

Go through it anyway.

You will put on newer, healthier spiritual clothing. Think of a snake that sheds its skin. It has to get rid of the old skin, the old layers, as it evolves and grows. The old skin doesn't fit anymore. It's worn and damaged and affords the snake less protection.

Such is the case with your old ways of navigating life. You must embrace this withdrawal with a spirit of acceptance and readiness. Allow yourself to lean into the grief, knowing that healing and growth lie on the other side. And remember that you are transforming into a healthier, more enhanced version of yourself that is in alignment with your divine purpose.

You have to tear down old defenses and build newer, more effective ones. The idea of defense mechanisms is very familiar in my line of work. We talk about psychological defenses such as resistance, anger, avoidance, passive-aggressive behavior, etc. We all have them. They usually originate for a reason. When we reflect on how we developed our attitudes and behaviors, we can usually point to influences or experiences from our past that helped shape who we are today. Oftentimes, ineffective defenses in the present started as effective defenses against pain in the past. Far removed from the painful event, yet still holding the same defenses, we are no longer protected. In fact, these old defenses are limiting us. Thus, opening those scars, tearing down old emotional walls, and breaking through old habits are physical experiences. It is a spiritual detox that feels like the flu. You will get the shakes. You will sweat it out. You will fall on your knees crying and praying in the midst of sleepless nights. At times, you may feel like you're going crazy. The people around you may start to notice changes. They may ask questions or start to treat you differently. They won't be able to make sense of what's happening to you. This is okay. Be patient with them. Establish the boundaries you need so that your shedding will not be interrupted. This is simply part of the process. It has to happen, and it is for your good.

The good news: Withdrawal doesn't last forever. The pain and discomfort are only temporary. There are things you can do to mitigate the pain, such as prayer, meditation, or seeking counsel from trusted sources.

But you still have to go through the process. You cannot avoid it or pass it along to someone else. Think of it as growing pains. We go through this during adolescence. Acne, hormonal changes, disproportions in our body, our first blush at romance—all of it. And most of it is uncomfortable. We do not forsake the growth simply because it's difficult or unpleasant.

Such is the case as you grow in understanding of self. Listen to your inner wisdom, and make the right choices. The withdrawal is only a signal. It is either a signal that you're getting rid of something that needs to go, or a signal that you've left something you need to return to. It's designed to help you advance to a higher level of creation. You will understand the nature of the withdrawal as you direct your focus inward. Your mind, body, and spirit will speak to you along this journey toward purpose. The messages will make sense. They will lead you to a truth only you will understand. Do not hold on to those things that are destined to be left behind. Withdrawal is not something to be feared. You have access to divine support at all times. You will lack nothing. You are evolving into a higher, truer expression of yourself with each step. You will emerge victorious. And You are not alone.

PURPOSE IN PRACTICE

- You experience withdrawal when you drift away from your divine purpose.
- Growth requires shedding old layers and letting go. This may not always feel good. There may be feelings of loss and grief even as you're progressing toward a better version of yourself.
- The things that we rely on for security—money, relationships, the approval of others—can eventually become our prisons. Don't let external comforts become internal confinements. Let go of artificial defenses, and embrace freedom by being fully present and open.

FOR YOUR YOUNGER SELF

These eyes knew no shame.

These hands had not yet experienced the pain of weakness.

There was no such thing as failure.

Or insecurity.

Or doubt.

Or comparison.

The world was kind, and loving, and generous.

It was inviting—and called us to play, and explore, and believe in the magic of life.

And then what happened?

We became afflicted by the not-good-enough disease and began to dine at the table of fear.

We were cautioned not to take risks. To play it safe. To make our dreams more "realistic."

We began to limit our résumés before we ever entered the workforce.

And we began to exist rather than live.

My dear friends, I'm here to remind you that you are more.

You are more than your fears, mistakes, assumptions, and limitations. You are even more than your current successes.

You were born with a purpose that only you can fulfill. And all the tools you need are already inside of you.

If you have dreams and passions that you are not pursuing, you are a thief. You are robbing this world of the gifts it needs and deserves. You cannot pass this responsibility to someone else. It is yours to complete.

This message is for you. Let's share in the magic that once was, and still is.

It's time to return to the unrestricted power and belief we were born with.

It's time to return to the wisdom of our youth.

Chapter Seven

Refills

---

*"But those who hope in the Lord will renew
their strength; They will soar on wings like
eagles; they will run and not grow weary, they
will walk and not be faint." ~ The Holy Bible.
Isaiah 40:31 (NIV)*

GROWTH AFTER DEATH

I magine being pronounced dead from a horrific car accident, and then waking up from a coma several weeks later.

This is the story of Hal Elrod. He was told by doctors that he would never walk again and that he had irreversible brain damage. He made an astounding recovery and went on to achieve massive success as an author and speaker. He writes about his experiences and strategies for perseverance in *The Miracle Morning*, which condenses the habits of highly successful individuals into a morning routine known as SAVERS: Silence (like prayer or meditation), Affirmations (speaking positive things into your life), Visualization (seeing yourself already having the things you desire), Exercise, Reading, and Scribing (like writing or journaling).

Hal would be the first to admit that the practices themselves are not new concepts. The revolutionary part is what happens when you put this combination into practice with intention over time. It's a catalyst for accelerating your path to self-improvement. *The Miracle Morning* movement has spread like wildfire. There is an international community of Miracle Morning practitioners around the globe who reach out to send words of inspiration and encouragement and share testimonies of how this practice has changed their lives.

But the important thing to remember is that doing SAVERS once or even a few times is not going to get you very far. You have to create a consistent habit. Refill your cup of motivation and purpose every single day. And the "miracle" truly lies in prioritizing the morning—the first part of our day that sets our minds and emotions in the healthiest frame possible to face whatever the day brings.

As we grow, we have to learn how and when to get more of what we need. This means asking for help effectively, reaching out for support, and anticipating when we run low on resources. These practices allow us to develop the patience to appreciate the cumulative effects of repeated effort over time.

Let's review the process of obtaining refills in the medical sense. Imagine you're seeing a doctor for treatment of high blood pressure. We all know that high blood pressure doesn't develop overnight, and, accordingly, it is not going to correct itself overnight. Therefore, we can't expect our blood pressure to be permanently under control after only one month of prescription medication. We will need to monitor our blood pressure and follow up with our doctor even if things appear stable. The principle of refills means going back to our physician and staying on the medication that got us healthy, as a means of remaining healthy. Similarly, in the journey of self-improvement, we have to return to our Source of purpose and engage in the right behaviors to reach our goals and achieve success.

So, just like getting that first prescription of blood pressure medication, we keep going back for more in order to stay on track. Maybe it's just a few months, a few years, or maybe it's the rest of your life that you're on this medication. This will be determined by the severity of your condition and the other risk factors that are associated with your illness. It's also contingent on the nature of your relationship with your physician. It requires staying compliant with treatment (which we touched on in a previous chapter), following up with appointments, and discussing what's working versus what needs to change. All of these things influence the duration of treatment and the experience of the doctor–patient relationship and healing.

CHECK YOUR CUP

Our emotional stamina for success is dependent on our getting refills appropriately. We have access to limitless supply through our Source. But we are also human. We have a finite amount of energy at any given point in time. So, we have to balance being judicious with our resources and returning for refills when we need them.

For many of us, this comes in the form of self-care: learning when to rest and recharge our batteries. It also involves knowing when to go back to our mentors or coaches for additional support. You may remember a favorite professor from college. There may have been a certain topic or assignment that you were struggling with; thus, you sought extra tutoring or support. It may have taken the form of one-on-one sessions with your professor, working with his or her assistant, or attending study hall. But how nice was it when that professor heard you, validated your concerns, and generously offered to help? You didn't have to be afraid or feel like a burden, or second-guess whether they would take your request seriously. You knew they had time for you, and they made your success a priority.

Such is our relationship with our Higher Power on this journey. He makes our growth and contentment a priority. He freely invites us to seek refills on the resources He supplies so we can get to the next level of purpose and enlightenment.

Of course, one of the prerequisites for getting a refill is knowing when you're running low on a resource. This principle seems obvious but is essential to keep in mind. When taking medication, you count your tablets along the way and anticipate when you're about to run out. Similarly, you track your progress as you pursue goals and recognize when you are coming up on a shortage or deficiency. We have to anticipate and pay attention. And rather than risk running out, we have to be proactive and reach out to our Provider ahead of time.

I can't tell you how many refill adventures I have with patients in my medical practice. There are those who are very responsible and let me know well ahead of when they actually run out of medication. I really appreciate this consideration. It makes my job easier and increases the likelihood of the patient's stability. They are more likely to remain well by taking an active part in their recovery and staying on top of medication issues or shortages. In contrast, there are those patients who aren't as mindful. They forget to keep track, or get distracted by other life problems, and suddenly realize they're on their last pill. In these instances, getting an urgent refill becomes a crisis for them—and an inconvenience for me. There's a similar process when you reach out to a coach or mentor at the last minute. No one likes a crisis. We perform better, and give better advice, when we have adequate time to think and prepare. When you create stress for the person helping you, it often clouds the relationship and makes the experience less productive.

Think of forgetting your refills like driving in heavy traffic. There's a lot of stopping and starting that is both frustrating and inefficient. You advance a little bit, then slow down, at times coming to a complete stop; you wait and then advance a little more. It's tiresome and often an uncomfortable ride. In contrast, driving on the open road is a much more pleasant experience. You can see ahead clearly, change lanes with ease, and set your own pace. You're much more likely to enjoy the ride and keep going. Such is the process when it comes to obtaining refills of purpose, ambition, and motivation well ahead of our shortages.

> **If we wait until we run out, we have to scramble to find more of what we need.**

We engage in the stop-start process, and it sets us back. We get frustrated, demoralized, and fatigued. We devalue our time and energy and don't demonstrate honor and gratitude for the Source of our supply. We have to remain mindful and intentional about anticipating problems and shortages, making sure to get refills in a timely manner.

SUCCESS LIES IN YOUR ROUTINE

There is no Easy-Bake Oven for success. Reaching our desired goals requires consistent effort and repetition. We can't base our decisions on our feelings and interests alone. I often think back to my days in medical training when I'm trying to encourage some of my younger patients who are frustrated with school or their first jobs after college. The path to becoming a physician is not a glamorous one. As a medical student, I had to do a lot of crap that I didn't want to do. There were many sleepless nights, challenging patients, bureaucracy in hospitals and academic institutions, and other hurdles that I had to face.

Early on, medical students are at the bottom of the totem pole and are expected not to complain. We have to write reports, give presentations, and seem enthusiastic about things that may not be our particular area of interest. Personally, I was never interested in working as an OB/GYN or trauma surgeon. But I still had to learn about those specialties, work with those patients, and give my best effort. That was part of my training, part of my commitment. And I would do it all over again. In life, we must do a lot of what we don't want to do, in order to do the things we want to do. There's no shortcut or magic formula here. You will encounter things that are boring, or uninteresting, or that you outright dislike during this journey. Do them anyway. And do them with your full effort and integrity.

This underscores the rationale of getting refills. No one loves the idea of taking medication, but we take it for the eventual benefits of healing and feeling better. Moreover, we acknowledge that taking medication once is probably not going to get the job done. Our health and our success are dependent on our ability to stay the course despite our feelings or circumstances.

There are many downstream benefits of consistency. Consider it a healthy side effect. The discipline required to take medication every day is also helping you stay organized and prioritize caring for your body. It will increase the likelihood of you making other health-promoting decisions, such as eating healthier foods, making time for exercise, reading about health principles, and keeping your doctor's appointments. There's a domino effect when it comes to healthy behaviors. They create a generative, compound effect that results in better outcomes than any of the individual behaviors could create on their own.

In simpler terms, the accumulation of little successes over time leads to massive success.

We often assume it's the other way around. But the truth is that it's not the one-time lottery win, six-figure sale, or big promotion that leads to greatness. Our success is a reflection of what we do every single day. It's a reflection of the habits we form and the small decisions we make repeatedly, accumulated over time, that ultimately lead to the goals we're trying to achieve. Don't complicate the process. You are working with a generous Source who specializes in abundance. You have access to an endless supply of everything that you need. You simply have to ask. And believe. And stay connected. Follow the directions on the bottle. Obtain refills when needed. The prescription was made just for you. You are already healing from within. And You are not alone.

PURPOSE IN PRACTICE

- Self-awareness includes knowing what you need when you need it. Become a better student of yourself, and tune in to what your inner spirit is asking.
- You cannot pour from an empty cup. Self-care is not selfish—it's essential. Find ways to give from a place of abundance instead of fatigue or obligation. You will be a healthier giver—and receiver—as a result.
- Medications for chronic conditions only work if you take them every day. Your life is a chronic

condition. You must do things every day that foster health and growth in order to achieve your ultimate purpose.

Chapter Eight

Changing Your Dosage

---

*"When you change the way you look at things,
the things you look at change." ~ Wayne Dyer*

THE MORNING AFTER

An integral part of residency training for physicians involves providing on-call coverage. Medicine is 24/7, and illness doesn't take days off. Despite advances in technology and remote care, there remains a need for onsite physicians at all times at most medical centers.

One of the ways on-call coverage was incentivized during my training was to offer paid shifts for senior residents. Every extra dollar helped those of us trying to chip away at student loan debt, and, in some cases, support a family. I was among those who didn't mind the work and would sign up for overnight shifts regularly. One of the more desirable locations was a psychiatric emergency room in downtown Philadelphia known as the Crisis Response Center (CRC). We saw everything there. There were well-to-do people from the community who were in the midst of situational crises sitting next to individuals who were brought in by police escort for acute psychosis.

As you can imagine, the overnight shift was particularly ripe with interesting cases. Frequently, our work in the CRC would come after a full day's work in the hospital or medical offices. We were tired. Worse was when we would have normal duties the next morning after an overnight shift. We had euphemisms such as "having a white cloud" or "pitching a no-hitter" to describe shifts that were particularly light and allowed for mostly uninterrupted sleep. One thing I remember vividly is the commute back home the mornings after those shifts. I would bundle up on the winter mornings, eyes half-glazed, and walk to the nearest metro station. It was surreal to see all the normal commuters bustling in—starched shirts, briefcases, and Starbucks in hand. I could feel their angst and hurriedness as they prepared for the day ahead. I felt like I was getting to "cheat" the traditional 9-to-5 paradigm, even if for a day.

My path looked different on those mornings. I got to prepare for rest as everyone else was preparing to work. I got a chance to slow down and let my brain be completely free. No obligations or expectations; nothing more to give of myself for that day. It was magic.

But I came to know that just because my day looked different didn't mean I wasn't on the same journey. I still had the same goals and ambitions. I was still moving toward the same destination—a fully licensed and practicing psychiatrist. Such is the origin of being stubborn with our goals but flexible with our path. Sometimes our conditions force us to change course. And that's okay, as long as you have an internal compass guiding you toward your goals.

This journey of self-improvement is about making adjustments. Change is the only constant that we can rely on. We have to make room for surprises, good and bad, and unexpected circumstances as we pursue our purpose. We cultivate flexibility in our decision-making and learn to pivot when life requires it. This speaks to the importance of anticipation and preparation. Preparation is an active process that reflects a set of behaviors and decisions that we carry out, usually for a known event or experience. It's the act of making a plan. When you know you have a test coming up, you prepare by reviewing your notes, hosting study groups, and getting adequate sleep the night before. Or when you have a big presentation to give at work, you start making your slides well ahead of time, fine-tuning them the week prior, and ideally having it polished days in advance of the meeting.

In both scenarios, you know what's ahead, and you know what's expected of you. Thus, the absence of preparation usually comes back to personal fault. Paraphrasing the words of Benjamin Franklin, "Those who fail to prepare are preparing to fail."

Anticipation, in contrast, is a bit more nuanced and requires a heightened level of awareness and attention.

Anticipation is a state of preparedness.

It involves the mental acuity and intuition to gauge what's around the corner and be ready for the not-fully-known.

Let's look at a sports analogy. When a quarterback throws a deep pass to his receiver, both parties attempt to anticipate what the other is going to do. Neither of them knows to perfection exactly what the other is going to do. There are some variables they won't know until the play starts. The quarterback, through experience and muscle memory, throws the ball with a precise amount of velocity, aim, and altitude. The receiver runs with a precise amount of speed and turns and extends his hands at the right time to catch the ball. Everything must happen in a certain sequence and harmony that is influenced by the laws of anticipation. So, even when you prepare, you must also learn to anticipate those things that we cannot fully know ahead of time.

We cannot get too comfortable or too confident or assume that things will always proceed as planned. We must marry preparation and anticipation when it comes to working toward personal goals, addressing limiting beliefs, or changing our habits. We must plan and adjust.

YOUR EMOTIONAL BUDGET

Changing our dosage also includes the process of "dialing it down," or knowing when to modulate our energy and effort. Many of us, including myself, struggle with the trap of perfectionism. We have lofty and oftentimes unrealistic expectations, and we fail to exercise sufficient patience and compassion toward ourselves. We have to remember that we are energetic beings and that energy is limited in the physical sense. In the same way that our cars run out of gas and we need to refuel, such is the case for our bodies and minds. We need time to recharge. You will not be able to give 100 percent every day—and that's okay. Your best will look different depending on the circumstances. You may just be getting over a cold, or going through a financial hardship, or changing relationships, or switching job situations, etc. You may only have 40 percent left in the tank. So the expectation is that you give 100 percent of that 40 percent to your most important priorities, and you make sure your personal well-being is at the top of that list.

In many ways, our emotional energy is like money. Meet John (a fictional character). John is married, has a four-year-old son, and works long hours at a job that he is not super enthused about. (Sound familiar?) John gets up on Monday morning and starts his day with $50 worth of emotional energy. He hits the snooze button one too many times on his phone, so now he's running late. That's $10 worth of energy he spends on panic for his potential tardiness. As he's driving, there's an accident ahead, so he uses an app to find a faster route— only to find that he's stuck behind everyone else who had the same idea. That's another $10 in frustration and mild road rage. When he gets to the office, he immediately spends $5 on a fake smile toward a coworker he doesn't actually like; $7 on boredom in a meeting during which they talk about the same issues they covered in the last three meetings; and another $10 scanning job websites during his lunch break, praying he comes across another opportunity that will help him escape his misery. John comes back home with only $8 left in his emotional wallet, a scarce amount to divide amongst his wife, son, and himself. Far too often, this "fake" illustration is a very real experience for many of us. We expend so much energy on the things we don't want and have very little left for the things that actually give us fulfillment. We have to be intentional about our priorities and take inventory of who or what is getting our best selves.

Another important feature to keep in mind about changing our dosage is leaving room for change within. We are dynamic, evolving beings that live in a dynamic, evolving world. Nothing about our inner or outer reality is static. Your journey toward self-development, your goals, and the process by which you pursue those goals will inevitably change along the way.

There are many different paths that lead to success. Having a flexible mindset along the way makes the process more tolerable and more enjoyable. It also leaves us open to more possibilities for how we can arrive at our goal.

Imagine we're traveling from Georgia to California. There are multiple modes of transportation that could get us there. We could take a car and drive across the country, which might take three or four days. We could get on a plane, which may take three or four hours. We could get on a train, or do a bicycle tour across the United States, which could take weeks or even months. You get the point—there are multiple paths leading to the same destination. If we start on one path, that doesn't exclude us from being able to change paths or priorities along the way. We have to value the journey and the destination equally and leave room for change in both.

THE LITTLE ENGINE THAT COULDN'T

In an earlier chapter, I cautioned against overdosing on success, so that we don't experience burnout before we reach our goals. But we also don't want to "underdose." If we put in too little effort or engagement, that will limit us as well. Small effort equals small results; big effort leads to big results. We don't want to give less than we are able to simply for the sake of conservation. Idle time is the breeding ground for procrastination, avoidance, self-doubt, and distraction. When we slow down unnecessarily, it sets us up for self-imposed obstacles. We should always give 100 percent when we are capable of doing so.

There's a popular quote that says, "Success loves speed," meaning, the faster we can turn our ideas into action and get some momentum behind what we're pursuing, the more likely we are to have the energy to sustain it along the way. Thus, we must be intentional about giving our best effort and increasing our dosage when we can. Moreover, we want to be strategic with how we do this.

> **The journey of living in our purpose is a marathon, not a sprint.**

It's similar to college. It takes four years to get a college degree, but there are some rewards and milestones along the way, which help incentivize us to keep going. If we're giving constant effort with no reward, it's hard to sustain that effort for very long. We are motivated by two primary objectives in life: seek pleasure and avoid pain. That's why it's important to celebrate small wins, make time for rest, diversify our activities, and, perhaps most importantly, remember to *play*.

We often see "playtime" as something incompatible with adulthood—and we couldn't be more mistaken. Your soul is replenished when you play. Find time to laugh, savor a new food, put your toes in the grass, trade silly memes with friends, play with your kids, and tickle your romantic partner. You have to keep *living* as you grow. As humans, we have an innate need to feel seen, heard, valued, and connected. It's okay to have fun. It's okay to seek acknowledgement and validation sometimes.

> **You have permission to feel good in the service of personal growth.**

Lastly, learn to expect the unexpected. There will be times when you are forced to stop and put the torch down temporarily. Life happens. You lose your job, a loved one dies, a romantic partner leaves, or a child goes wayward. It's okay to press pause on your ambitions in these moments of distress. Those are not the times to beat yourself up for adjusting your timeline or shifting your priorities.

We have to remain flexible in the service of survival and life management. We must balance compassion and reason throughout the process. The success process comes in phases. So, instead of the high-energy phase where you're building, pursuing, selling, networking, etc., you may transition back to a low-energy phase such as brainstorming, reflecting, or jotting down ideas as they come. All of this is okay.

> **Your goals are meaningless without self-preservation.**

Once the dust settles and you are in a more stable emotional state, you can return to the active, high-energy phase. We must crave patience as much as we crave results. Your dreams will not escape you as long as you remain connected to the Source. He will provide all you need at any point in time. Be trusting as He is trusting. Be faithful as He is faithful. Remember that this life was already predetermined with your success in mind. You are growing in wisdom and clarity each day. You are attracting goodness and abundance into your life. You are reason enough to pursue greatness. You are love. And You are not alone.

PURPOSE IN PRACTICE

- Be stubborn about your goals but flexible about your path. Being able to pivot is a critical skill for overcoming unexpected challenges.

- Treat your emotional energy like money. You only have a finite amount to spend each day. Choose wisely. Don't go into emotional debt over low-value frustrations.

- You hold the remote for your life. Remember to Play. Know when to Pause. Maybe even Stop. Oh … and one more thing: Don't waste time with the Rewind or Fast-Forward buttons. They don't work.

Chapter Nine

Brand Name Medically Necessary

"We are what we repeatedly do. Excellence, therefore, is not an act, but a habit." ~ Aristotle

YOU ARE BEING SOLD

We live in an age of consumerism. Companies are constantly vying for our attention and, more importantly, our wallets. I'm writing this chapter on the day of the Super Bowl, during which a 30-second TV ad costs $5 million.

Yes, you read that correctly.

What's even more mind-boggling is that companies actually spend that amount because they expect to make more on the back end in sales revenue. They have stud-

ied our behaviors and spending patterns. Ads are ubiqui-
tous on our news feeds and social media pages, and the
things we look for on search engines are tracked. We are
being sold to all the time. Marketing and branding is a
science. We identify certain brands with status and success, and they have become household names. When you
want to blow your nose, you ask for a Kleenex. When
you want to photocopy something, you make a Xerox.
Want to look something up online? Google it. Brands
have shaped our culture and literally changed our lan-
guage. This is the power of influence, and the same principles apply as we move toward our goals.

We must understand the importance of our reputa-
tions—our personal brands—as we strive toward growth
and self-improvement. Our self-assessment will only
take us so far. Our character affects our success, both
how we are perceived by the outside world and how we
choose to engage behind closed doors. We must show up
with integrity at all times.

Showing up with integrity means being selective
with the things we expose ourselves to along this journey of personal improvement. The Buddha once said,
"What we think we become." And what we consume
we become as well. We are, in fact, a reflection of the
company we keep. We must be intentional with who we
allow into our inner circle. This involves prioritizing our
emotional safety and having values and boundaries that

help us navigate interactions with others. We have to pay attention to who has access to the most intimate parts of our lives, how they got there, and whether they have kept our trust to remain there.

> **We also have to be purposeful about feeding our minds and bodies things of high quality.**

We grow when we surround ourselves with people, places, and things that add value to our lives. It's okay to have high standards and expectations for ourselves and others. It means investing in ourselves and paying the premium for higher quality resources and experiences. If you cut corners, you are more likely to incur more costs and risks down the road. We need to affirm that we are deserving of the best.

Let's explore this in the medical sense. In an earlier chapter, we talked about finding the right treatment for our problems and afflictions. Very commonly, when someone is taking a prescription medication, that medication is available in both brand name and generic form. When a pharmaceutical company first makes a medication, it secures a patent on that medication and has exclusive rights to be its only manufacturer for a number of years. The medication is given a brand name, and this allows the pharmaceutical company to establish market presence and familiarity with consumers. This is particularly relevant now in the age of direct-to-consumer marketing. Name recognition and brand loyalty form the golden goose that each of these companies strives for. This keeps their name in our minds and their hands in our wallets. I don't mean to sound cynical, but medicine is a business, and there are legitimate reasons for this. The process of drug development and FDA approval can be very costly for the pharmaceutical companies.

After a number of years, the exclusivity is lifted, and it opens opportunity for other pharmaceutical companies to create a nearly identical product. These are the principles of competition in a free-market society. And I say *nearly identical* product in the sense that the generic form may not be exactly the same as the original brand name. There are some specific parameters that the FDA allows in terms of variance from the brand-name chemical. There is some percentage of variability in the amount of the active ingredient in a generic formulation versus a brand name. Additionally, even if the active ingredient is the same amount and the same potency, sometimes there are different additives or fillers the generic manufacturers use to package the medication. This may differ from what the original company was using for the brand name, which isn't necessarily cause for alarm. More often than not, the effectiveness of a generic medication is comparable to that of the brand name. The lesson here is once something deviates from its original condition, there are other factors to consider. It requires a level of thoughtfulness and discernment to know what those differences are and their potential implications. Conversely, when you invest in a brand, you know what you're getting every time. There will be times in your journey toward purpose where it will be well worth your effort to invest in proven, brand-name resources.

You can't put a price tag on your peace of mind.

We have to choose our associations carefully and represent our personal brand with integrity. It can be to our advantage to invest in resources that have stood the test of time. We know these resources and others have vetted them already.

Let's look at an example of this in the fast-food industry. When you go to a Burger King in Atlanta versus a Burger King in Chicago, you have some confidence that your experiences will be similar. There's enough consistency in the menu to know that a Whopper in Atlanta and a Whopper in Chicago are going to have the same toppings, the same quality of meat, and the same preparation pattern. It's a standardized product. However, we can't have the same level of confidence in comparing a Whopper in Atlanta with a hamburger from "John Doe's Burgers" in Nowhereville, USA. There is no assurance that the quality of the product or experience of the service is going to be the same.

This whole idea of branding is that you're giving your customers some assurance that they are going to get a consistent, high-quality product or service. Thus, we need to be consuming consistent, high-quality resources in order to develop ourselves into consistently high-achieving, high-quality human beings. This applies to the books we read, podcasts we listen to, videos we watch, and conferences we attend. It is also reflected in the mentorship and coaching we receive and the environments we put ourselves in every day.

And I'm not here to pretend this is free. There is a cost to these things. We can either look at that cost as an expense … or an investment. The rewards may not be immediate, but we understand the value of what we are pursuing and what we are purchasing in the service of personal growth. I'll admit, I've been guilty of going about this the wrong way. I have tried to pinch pennies on the front end and, more often than not, I ended up paying more in the long run. My wife likes to remind me of this frequently. As an example, there have been times in the past when I've insisted on taking a flight with layovers for the purpose of saving on the cost of airfare. My wife is a firm believer in flying nonstop whenever possible. Well, wouldn't you know that on more than one occasion, my cheaper ticket resulted in unexpected delays, missed connections, and priceless I-told-you-so looks from my better half. What I thought was "a deal" financially ended up costing us more in the travel experience.

Now, I'm not suggesting that you go blow your bank account on personal development resources. I am saying prioritize this process as an investment. Put it in your budget. Have a portion reserved for self-development in the same way you have a portion for groceries, car payments, cell phones, etc. Perhaps you're saying, "I can't afford this."

I say you can't afford not to.

Maybe that means just $10 a month right now, but $10 a month might buy you one self-help book. Or $10 a month over the course of a year might cover your registration fee for a personal-development seminar you want to attend. It's about being intentional and cultivating the mindset that you deserve high-quality information and experiences.

Now is the time to get clear on your ethics and values if you haven't already. What are your standards? What is your vision for yourself? What are the characteristics of the person you are aiming to become? Knowing the answers to these questions will help define your vision and purpose. Simon Sinek, author and social psychologist, has popularized the principle of finding our "Why." Your "Why" is your reason for taking this journey in the first place. It's what motivates you, inspires you, and keeps you going when things get tough. Your "Why" may change over time, but it is a core component of what sustains you through challenges and discouragement. It is inevitable that we will face hardships and have setbacks. It has to happen. There may be financial challenges, life events, and other circumstances that affect the amount of time or the pace with which you are able to pursue this journey.

But don't compromise your standards just because it might be easier or more convenient. Hold firm to your values.

Because that's what defines integrity.

And integrity is key for your long-term growth and success.

VALUES INFLUENCE RESULTS

The more we cut corners, the more we set ourselves up for disappointment and failure. We will never enjoy the process or achieve the outcomes we desire if we live without integrity.

It's a lot like building a house. A good house starts with laying a solid foundation. And then there are stabilizing structures such as flooring and load-bearing walls. We need duct work for ventilation and wiring for electricity. And, on the outside, we need sturdy siding and a good roof to protect us from the elements. We also secure our valuables with locks on the doors and alarm systems. No one wants unwelcome intruders. If we start compromising in any of these areas, e.g., getting cheap lumber, using old shingles, not paying attention to the fit of bolts and screws—we are more likely to have problems later on.

These same principles apply to your standards and values. Pay attention to the details. Make sure they are airtight. When we compromise our integrity, we become exposed. That exposure may show up as dishonesty, manipulation, blame, or hypocrisy. Any of those things can create leaks in our character.

Leaks in our character are difficult to repair.

A colleague at work refers to me as Spider-Man because of my "sixth sense" and intuition. There are times during our team discussions when my gut instinct tells me something isn't quite right. Maybe it's a patient who hasn't told us the full story. Or maybe there's a lab test we need to check, other medical records to review, or someone we need to speak with to get more information about the patient. It's always something. I'll let the group know that "my Spidey sense is tingling." They'll chuckle appropriately, but they also realize that further investigation is warranted. Some will even nod affirmatively that they had a similar feeling, too.

This is no accident. Intuition is an energy that can be shared and transmitted collectively. And, sure enough, at some later point, we'll get the rest of the story that confirms our hunch.

I apply this same intuition in my personal life. There are times when I pause or hesitate to do something. I try to avoid making decisions, saying things, or going places that don't *feel* right. The reason for the hesitation usually isn't revealed until after the fact. This spirit of discernment is something I hold in high regard and has been developed through my intentional practice of listening and observing. My sense of awareness grows as I make time daily for quiet reflection, going within, and consulting with my Creator on all things of significance.

You have the ability to develop your gifts as well.

We all have an inner wisdom guiding us. Train yourself to recognize it. Listen to it. Stay true to your God-given values and gifts. Remember that you were made from the finest ingredients in the Universe. You deserve the best of what life has to offer. You are living on purpose with a purpose. You are God's favorite brand. And You are not alone.

PURPOSE IN PRACTICE

- You are what you consume. Learn to be selective about what you expose yourself to.
- Too often we undervalue what we need. It's okay to invest in high-quality resources for your growth. You are absolutely worth it!

- Your true character is who you are when no one is looking. Be your best self for you, not for anyone else.

THE GOOD SURGEON

Open heart surgery.

Not the medical kind that involves operating rooms, doctors, and scalpels, etc.

But the spiritual kind.

The kind that involves a change from deep within.

The kind we all have to go through in order to grow and unlock our full potential in life.

In some ways, the process is similar to medical surgery.

Before you go under the knife, you meet with your surgeon for a pre-op evaluation.

During this time, they'll perform a physical exam, check bloodwork, and run other tests—like an EKG or a CT scan.

They'll get an assessment of your overall health to see if you're a good candidate for surgery. To make sure you're aware of the risks. To inform you of what behaviors and habits will need to change. To make sure it's safe to proceed.

That last point is crucial—to make sure it's safe to proceed.

A good surgeon will pay particular attention to this part.

You have to be willing.

And if you didn't already know, the surgery itself is no walk in the park.

You're put to sleep. The surgical site (where the incision takes place) is cleaned and prepped. They'll cut through skin, muscle, blood vessels, and nerves. Your rib cage is retracted open to expose the heart. The area of disease is identified and removed.

The surgery itself doesn't feel good. You're in pain. Your chest is sore. It may hurt to cough, or bend ... or even laugh as you recover.

But there is healing on the other side.

Perhaps you are in need of open heart surgery.

You may have some habits, some people in your life, some masks you wear that you thought were "protecting" you. But all they're doing is concealing the blockage on the inside and keeping the disease within.

If you're looking for a good surgeon, I may have a referral. He's the best in the Universe. His technique is precise. He will leave no scar. He's got the best credentials. And He's never lost a case.

Chapter Ten

Safe Disposal

"If you want to awaken all of humanity, then awaken all of yourself. If you want to eliminate the suffering in the world, then eliminate all that is dark and negative in yourself. Truly, the greatest gift you have to give is that of your own self-transformation." ~ Lao Tzu

EXCESS BAGGAGE

Gary Vaynerchuk, affectionately known as "Gary Vee" to his tribe of followers, is a powerhouse on social media. He made a name for himself growing his father's wine business, and then skyrocketed to his own success in the world of marketing and brand management. He has a crass, no-nonsense style that emphasizes putting in the work and not hiding behind complaints or excuses. He espouses deploying massive amounts of patience and empathy as you hustle toward your goals, selling the value of self-sacrifice and delayed gratification.

Beneath the sting and sizzle of his words is a message of genuine positivity. He prioritizes happiness above all else. Gary admonishes us to tune out the internalized voices in our heads (e.g., parents, teachers, spouses) that may have good intentions but are ultimately keeping us from following our dreams. He notes that it's often the fear of judgment from people we care about that holds us back from pursuing our truest desires.

I consume a lot of Gary's content and had the pleasure of seeing him speak at a live event in 2017. He is steady as an arrow and hammers the same message consistently. I use him to frame the core message of this chapter: Get rid of negativity at all costs.

Many of our burdens are self-imposed.

We may not have chosen our problems, but often we are choosing to keep them. We complain, bring up the past, wallow in self-pity, focus on what we lack, and, ultimately, stop trying. We add bricks of negativity into the luggage we drag around every day. And we wonder why we're tired, sore, unhappy, and not progressing. We have to find a way to remove the dead weight—quickly and permanently.

Perhaps, as a divine coincidence, my heart was heavy as I was initially writing this chapter. I learned that a classmate of mine from college died unexpectedly. His name was Michael. He left behind a wife and two young children. He was a close friend to my wife and genuinely a good person. We attended each other's weddings and celebrated each other's personal and professional achievements, even though we were separated by time and distance. Michael was a leader and an influencer. I don't recall ever hearing him complain or speak negatively. I know he was human and had his shortcomings just like anyone else, but he was intentional with how he presented himself. He was a caring and committed man who always had a positive attitude. He was generous with his support and touched many lives in meaningful ways.

My wife was able to attend his funeral and remarked at the large number of people in attendance. Everyone was grieving in disbelief at the tragic realization that Michael was gone. That really put things into perspective for me. Here was a guy, like me, in the prime of his life who had achieved a high level of success by many accounts. He was living with purpose and had a keen awareness of what really mattered. And then it was over—without warning or preparation. In the wake of this untimely news, I stopped to reflect on a few important questions that were swirling in my mind:

What legacy am I creating?

How will I be remembered?

Am I using my gifts to the best of my ability?

To find the answers, I had to take inventory of what I was carrying. I realized that I needed to get rid of some things that were hindering me from fully living in my purpose. There were some habits, emotions, and memories that were getting in the way of my growth. They all had to go. I knew I had gifts to share with the world. And Michael's loss was a grim reminder that tomorrow isn't promised.

> **We cannot afford to hide behind excuses, blame, or circumstances to justify why we are not achieving greatness.**

Life is not guaranteed to any of us, and we have no time to waste on negativity. We must commit to finding the good in life, particularly during hard times. It's okay to grieve. It's okay to feel bad. And it's okay to make mistakes. But we cannot stay there. We have to honor the "Why" that gives us a reason to continue this journey each day.

WASH YOUR (EMOTIONAL) HANDS

So, let's explore how we get rid of emotional baggage and negative energy along our journeys of self-transformation. We begin by identifying ways to cleanse ourselves physically, emotionally, and spiritually. We have to find the right places to leave our problems so that we don't pick them back up or risk them falling into the hands of others who mean us harm.

Some of you have experienced the latter. Sadly, there are people who don't want to see us succeed. They wait for opportunities to air our dirty laundry, spread rumors, or use our shortcomings against us. Don't be discouraged by these people. Michael Beckwith says, "Mediocrity always attacks excellence." These people are simply acting out of their own pain and limitations.

Here's a medical analogy for the sake of illustration: Imagine you have a supply of unused medication that you need to dispose of. It isn't safe to keep it around. Your kids may get into it. Or maybe a nosy guest. Or you may get confused and take the wrong medication by accident. For these reasons and others, we conclude that it is best to get rid of it. Well, you're not supposed to flush medication down the toilet or pour it down the drain. It may contaminate the water supply. Even worse is throwing away unused medication. There is an unsavory practice of people going through trash looking for unused medications to take or sell illicitly. It is necessary to be discreet and thoughtful about how we dispose of these things.

The same themes apply for getting rid of negative emotional baggage. Just substitute "problems" for "medications." They can be secrets, mistakes, insecurities, or old beliefs. At some point, you will have an excess supply that you need to dispose of. You need to get rid of old ways in order to make room for new opportunities, but you must do this safely. Be cautious about whom you vent to or share negative information with. This is not only to protect you from those who aim to take advantage of you but also to ensure that you don't negatively impact others. We have to be good stewards of our negative energy and find safe outlets so that we don't contaminate someone else's health.

I have been guilty of this at times, and I hear the same thing from my friends and colleagues. We have all been exposed to rumors and gossip that we would prefer not to hear. Pain is an energy that leads to unrest, and often it cannot be contained in one form for too long. We grow unsettled keeping pain inside and we look for ways to release it. If we're not careful, we can make the error of passing that pain to others inappropriately.

We feel an unconscious need to get rid of pain. We want to shed the discomfort and have other people validate how we feel. We want to feel justified and acknowledged. We are right, and the person who hurt us is wrong—or so goes the narrative we create as a bandage for our wounds.

This process of transferring pain may end up trapping us more than the person we feel wronged us. We are the ones holding on to the negative energy, the painful narrative, repeating and rehashing the story until we get the comfort and validation we seek. It can be a tireless endeavor. Also, we are likely contaminating others along the way.

The friend we are venting to may have been having a good day prior to encountering us. They were happy, their energy was positive, and then here we come, guns blazing with negativity. "OMG, you won't believe what happened to me today!" And we start dumping on them emotionally without invitation. We get into all the details of how somebody hurt us, how unfair the world is, and everything else that is wrong in our lives. We want to exchange our pain for their comfort.

That's not a very fair trade.

Our negative energy is the dominant force in that moment. It will overpower them if they are unprepared. We are more likely to bring our friend down than to get the relief we are seeking.

This is primarily because the healing we seek is from within. It can't be found in the outside world. There's a popular adage that says it takes five positive experiences to override one negative experience. I can't speak to the science of this statement, but there is good sense in it. From an evolutionary standpoint, our brains are hardwired for survival. We are primed to recognize threats and negative stimuli in our environments. We build our defenses around this psychology and educate our young to avoid danger more than we encourage them to seek opportunities for growth. Thus, we have a natural bias to recognize and magnify negativity over positivity. We have to be intentional in overriding this biological feedback loop. Unfortunately, the world we live in doesn't help. We are bombarded with negativity. You turn on the news, and it's fears about the economy, someone's been shot, a politician is engaging in corrupt behavior, or some other example of injustice in the world. It's hard to pull ourselves out of this saturation.

PERMISSION GRANTED

Sadly, negativity is part of the fabric of our culture, but we have a responsibility to manage and remove our own. It's okay to lean on family and close friends, but we need to dedicate a time and space for that. And we also need the other person's consent.

Too often, we end up blindsiding our loved ones with our complaints and negativity to the point of distancing them from us. They feel burdened and overwhelmed by our emotional pain, which then adds new pain and tension to the relationship. We end up arguing with the very person we were initially seeking comfort from. So, we need to schedule a time and place for more difficult conversations. This gives the other person time to prepare mentally and emotionally, decreasing the chances of them resenting us.

You also have to set some ground rules. You need to be willing to respect their boundary for how much of your negativity they can tolerate at any given time. They are not your emotional garbage disposal. Help them help you. And be particularly mindful sharing your pain with "friends" on social media. I use quotations there purposely. Too many of us are disseminating our pain to the masses and expecting relief. We go on long rants about how we were mistreated, dissatisfied with a company's product or service or our terrible boss or coworker, or why we're breaking up with our significant other. We turn into "keyboard warriors" and demand justice in the court of public opinion. Unfortunately, that only opens us up for more pain. We end up reading comments that we disagree with, or we feel upset by internet trolls who simply want to stir the pot and cause strife online. We take what they say personally, or worse, lash out by responding to them and opening a new wound.

We step away from the computer after the damage is done, and the emotions of guilt, shame, and regret soon follow when we realize the implications of what we've shared indiscriminately. What you put into the Universe, online or otherwise, will come back to you—the Law of Attraction at its core.

Once you get negativity out, you want to leave it somewhere where you're not likely to pick it back up. Let's try a visualization exercise. Imagine you have one of those large, black plastic lawn-and-garden bags. There is a sticker on the outside of the bag labeled "emotional waste." Imagine filling that bag with all of your negative energy and then leaving it in your bedroom next to your bed. It starts to stink pretty quickly, and you realize you are setting yourself up for a mess. You see it every day, may be tempted to open it back up, see what you put in there, or pick it back up and carry it with you. It's going to be part of your everyday life all over again. Even though you bagged up the negativity, you didn't actually get rid of it.

In comparison, let's say you take that same bag, fill it with negativity, and then set it on the curb on trash day. Clearly, this is a more effective plan. The garbage men are coming to collect it and take it away, so you don't have to deal with it again. This drives home the point that we need to be mindful and purposeful when we are trying to shed a bad habit or get rid of negative energy. We have to be able to get it out and leave it out. We have to walk away from it, not pick it back up, and not put it in other parts of our lives where we're going to be exposed to it again. In the trash bag analogy, you must make sure you're leaving it on the curb on the right day—the day when the trash man is coming.

If not, you run the risk of someone else, perhaps with bad intentions, coming across it and going through your emotional garbage. These are people who thrive on negativity. They specialize in closet skeletons and dirty laundry. So, we have to be discerning about where we leave our negative baggage physically, emotionally, and spiritually.

THE PROCESS OF SAFE DISPOSAL

Here are a few safe outlets to dispose of negative energy:

- Spiritual: yoga, meditation, spend time in nature, attend church, participate in a small group, confide in a priest or spiritual mentor
- Physical: exercise, aromatherapy, reflective breathing, leisure activities (e.g., date night, watching a funny movie, playing games with friends)
- Emotional: journal, attend a support group, work with a doctor or therapist, repeat daily affirmations, listen to inspirational music, engage in service or giving to others.

Similar to most strategies that work, these ideas and activities are not a one-time fix. We have to build a tool kit of resources and behaviors we can turn to when we need to dispose of negativity. You will fill up multiple trash bags of negative energy throughout this journey. Stay vigilant and proactive about your negativity meter.

Take inventory of negativity in the same way you do in your home. Think of it as emotional "spring cleaning." We tidy up our emotions in the same way we tidy our homes. It can be a very cleansing and liberating experience, but it takes work.

In our homes, we often accumulate more stuff than we need. We have to assess what's no longer needed, what no longer fits, and what's just taking up space. If the things we find still have value for someone else, we give them away. If it's just junk, we throw it away.

In the same way, we get to throw away our negative experiences and limiting beliefs. They no longer have a place in our lives, and they are contaminating us. Dr. Wayne Dyer said, "No one ever died from a snakebite. It's the venom that continues to circulate that eventually kills you."

> **We are holding emotional venom inside, and it will eventually kill us.**

We have to let it go and make room for the antidote, to create space for health and new energy. Don't give emotional space to things that don't belong. There is no vacancy for negativity in your life. You don't need it. It's not for you to keep. Your Designer has far greater things in store for your life. You deserve only good. And You are not alone.

PURPOSE IN PRACTICE

- Take inventory of the things you're carrying. We may not choose our problems, but often we hold on to excess baggage of negative emotions and memories for too long.

- Learn to release your pain in thoughtful ways. Don't transfer it to people you love without warning and expect them to hold what you couldn't. You'll end up creating a new problem in the process.

- When you let pain go, let it go completely. Seal the bag tightly, take it to the dumpster, and don't turn back.

Chapter Eleven

Proper Storage

"Lots of people want to ride with you in the limo,
but what you want is someone who will take the
bus with you when the limo breaks down."
~ Oprah Winfrey

UNDERSTANDING THE FRIEND ZONES

You have to know where people stand in your life. There are some friends who will be part of your inner circle while others remain peripheral. And you reserve the right to change their position at any time. You can adjust your boundaries and your degree of closeness with people in your life. Setting and adjusting boundaries is a part of healthy self-preservation. It's also the right thing to do for people you care about and respect. People need to know where they stand in your life. Without boundaries, we end up confusing people, and at times hurting them unintentionally. We sometimes get deceived into thinking that "walking on eggshells" or avoiding confrontation is the right thing to do. However, this usually ends up perpetuating discomfort, and it keeps us from building trust. Being clear in our communications and actions toward others shows them that we value their feelings and care enough to be open and honest with them.

The world deserves our authenticity.

This includes being honest about our desires, needs, and limits in relation to others. Bishop T.D. Jakes shares a wonderful illustration for how to assess and categorize the people in our lives. He begins with describing our confidants. These are the people who desire time with us. They trust us and are driven by their ability to interact with us. It is important to keep them in close proximity in order to retain them. If you give them a role away from you, they will likely leave. They care more about you as a person than they do the mission or task at hand.

Next, we have constituents. These people are dedicated to a shared goal more than the relationship with you. They will be loyal as long as the mission and purpose remain. Once the objective is complete, they are likely to leave. They are okay with working apart from you as long as they are tied to the mission at hand.

Lastly, Bishop Jakes describes comrades. These are people who join you because you have a common enemy. They are there for the fight and only the fight. You do not want to confide deeply in these people because they will turn on you when the fight is over. They are always looking for another conflict to rally to, and you may be the next one they attack.

It's important to recognize each of these types of people in your journey and learn how to work with all of them. You need each of them at some point. Don't resent the ones who eventually leave you. They were supposed to leave.

> **Some friends are for life, and some are just for a season.**

We have to be intentional about the people and environments we surround ourselves with. We have a responsibility to keep our ideas and dreams in a place where they are not subject to excessive scrutiny, discouragement, or corruption. We are made of energy. That energy is delicate and susceptible to influence, particularly in the early stages of our journeys. In the same way ice melts when exposed to heat, the nature of your dreams may change if subjected to extremes. Your internal talents and gifts were designed with specific parameters in mind. The gift of vision serves no purpose in total darkness. The gift of speech has no value if no one can hear. Thus, your responsibility is twofold: cultivate and master your gifts, and make sure you're using them in an environment where they can flourish.

The principle of proper storage involves remaining out of reach of negativity and having internal mechanisms for security and protection. And part of our armor comes from developing healthy habits and building an effective support system.

STAYING OUT OF REACH

Let's return to a medical analogy to describe the process of proper storage. Oftentimes, on the side of a medication bottle, there are instructions about how and where to store that medication. You may be advised to avoid extreme temperatures, such as the glove compartment of your car during the summertime. Chemicals are designed to be most active within a certain temperature range. By exposing one to higher or lower temperatures, there is the possibility of particles in the medicine disintegrating or changing their nature. The medication might lose its potency and effectiveness. It could even become harmful.

Another security measure for storing medication may be using a lockbox. This is particularly relevant with controlled substances such as narcotics. There may be wandering eyes and hands around these types of medications. And, equally often, those wandering eyes may be innocent if there are children or loved ones in the home who are curious about what's inside the medicine cabinet. Unfortunately, intent doesn't mitigate the potential for harm in this case. You don't want medications falling into the wrong hands. The same is true for our dreams and aspirations. Intent doesn't really matter.

Many of your critics have good intentions and are trying to guide or protect you with their advice. Their efforts can be harmful nonetheless. Feeling discouraged or scrutinized, second-guessing yourself, being advised to pursue a "more stable" path, leaving room for doubt … all of these things will slow you down and distract you from your inner wisdom. We must be careful whom and what we expose our ideas to. The energy of discouragement or regret is difficult to overcome.

Picture this scene: You've just returned from the grocery store with the ingredients for your favorite meal. The kitchen is cleaned and prepped, waiting for your culinary symphony to begin. You begin preparing the food. The spices are flowing, aroma fills the air, and your taste buds are dancing. You finish a delicious meal and have some leftovers. What are you going to do with those? Throw them out? Of course not! You put a lot of effort into preparing this meal, and you enjoyed the results. So, you're going to package the leftovers up carefully and store them in the refrigerator. You're not going to leave cooked food out overnight. You want to avoid the risk of bacteria or other contaminants that may spoil the food and make it unhealthy or unsafe to consume. And food is just one example. Many things in our everyday life require proper storage: medications, clothing, cosmetic products, vehicles, etc. I remember the winters from college in Michigan. There was no covered parking for students. There were many cold mornings when my car was covered with snow and had a sheet of ice on the windshield. That added an extra layer of inconvenience to my already hurried mornings. I didn't have the proper storage for my car in those conditions. And similarly, many of us are leaving our wishes and dreams out in the cold.

We need to be mindful about how we store ourselves and our gifts in the same way we're mindful of how we store products and possessions. Our dreams are not meant for everybody, particularly in their infancy. It's normal to be insecure early on. Ideas rarely come out fully formed when they begin. It makes sense to want feedback as we're mulling over an idea or a new goal. Perhaps you're just looking for validation or some reassurance that you're on the right track. That's okay. Just be mindful of who you turn to for consultation. You want to store that dream in a secure place and only allow access to people who are going to treat it responsibly and thoughtfully. You want to make sure they will follow your instructions for how to respond.

I'm sure you've seen those large crates that say "handle with care" in big red letters. Your life's purpose is in one of those crates. Handle it with care. Make sure those you invite to your inner circle do the same.

SELF-CARE ISN'T SELFISH

We've discussed how we store the invisible: our hopes, dreams, and ideas. Now let's talk about proper storage of the visible—in this case, our physical bodies.

The past two decades have brought tremendous insights into neuroscience and the mind–body connection. This is a highly intimate, integrated system. We know with certainty that our physical health affects our mental health and vice versa. So, we can have the best ideas in the world, but if we're not sleeping adequately, if we're not eating the right things, or if we're not exercising, those ideas aren't going to come to fruition as planned. Those dreams aren't going to manifest as effectively as they would if we were taking care of our bodies.

We have to be purposeful in how we care for our bodies, what environments we put our bodies in, and what substances and other things we consume. Garbage in, garbage out. I've personally cut back on watching unhealthy content on social media. There were fight videos and sexualized pictures that would pop up on my feed. I wouldn't even need to search for the stuff. The media says that "sex sells," but the question is: Who is profiting? I certainly didn't feel like I was. So, I made a change to be more deliberate and discerning with the content I consumed online.

We are not immune to the things we watch, listen to, touch, or taste. Our five senses were designed to protect us. Something that feels good may not actually be good for us.

I had to make binary decisions: Is consuming this content getting me closer to my goals, or is it keeping me where I am? That's it. I couldn't negotiate with my emotions. And I'm glad I made this new commitment to myself. The results have been amazing thus far. My thoughts are clearer, I have more energy, and I can sustain my focus for longer periods of time. Hence, how I finally moved from *thinking* to *doing* in writing this book.

Now, I'm not saying that my decisions are the standards for success. But I am encouraging you to take inventory of your patterns. If you're not where you want to be, make some different decisions. You may realize that what you're consuming, what you're storing inside of you, is not in alignment with your purpose.

This is a topic where size matters.

You want to keep big ideas away from small minds.

People who are small-minded—always negative, always pessimistic, always doubting—are not the people you want to surround yourself with or share your ideas with. Bad company corrupts good character. You're more likely to become discouraged if you filter through their negativity than you are likely to benefit from their feedback. It's just not worth it. And so we have to develop both internal and external mechanisms of protection. Make sure you have the right emotional armor. Put on defenses such as confidence, resilience, optimism, and faith so that you can handle the natural disappointments that are bound to occur. Sometimes it's necessary for us to defend against ourselves, too. We can be our own biggest critics, so being able to manage our inner voices is just as important as bracing against the winds of opposition from the outside—not only avoiding extremes in our environment but also avoiding extremes in our own behavior.

This is when we revisit the theme of authenticity. We have to avoid trying to be someone we are not. This includes overperforming or trying to copy someone else's path to success. Fully embrace and accept who you are, being cautious not to overuse modesty and humility.

Even good traits are best used in moderation.

Too much meekness and deference can be just as problematic as arrogance, or narcissism, or stubbornness.

In the same way we don't want to subject our medication bottles to extreme temperatures, we don't want to engage in extremes in our personalities, thoughts, or behaviors. We want to find a middle path that leaves room for self-expression but keeps a balance along the way. We have to remain mindful not to overdo any one aspect of ourselves. Our spirit will reward us when we treat our bodies and minds with compassion, kindness, and intentional care.

I'll reference Mel Robbins for a second time here because her insights are so profound. In *The 5 Second Rule*, she talks about being able to override our brain's natural tendency to magnify perceived threats. This is called the spotlight effect, i.e., shining a light on what our brain sees as potentially dangerous. Our brain's efforts to keep us safe can also keep us stuck and fearful of pushing toward change. *The 5 Second Rule* in practice interrupts this automatic mechanism and is a powerful tool to break negative thought loops. You choose a more positive, anchoring thought like "I'm okay" or "I am safe," count backward from five to one, and take action when you reach the number one. It's so simple but works like magic. Physiologically, you are moving from a more primitive part of the brain to the prefrontal cortex, which is responsible for planning and decision-making. You are moving from passive instincts to active intention. This is the core of developing discipline and healthy habits.

You are in alignment with your Creator when you act from a place of forethought and preparation. You must safeguard from both internal and external forms of negativity. We manage the internal by taking ownership of our thoughts. We have the ability to set the direction of our thoughts toward growth, health, and progress through the power of intention.

A thought is the most powerful energy in the universe. As humans, we were equipped with the gift of thought. Take pride in this. Your thoughts influence your decisions. You made a decision to improve your life. A decision to purchase this book. A decision to no longer settle. A decision to step into your divine purpose. Be proud of what you are pursuing. Don't let anyone convince you otherwise. You are stored on the highest shelf in God's cabinet. You are out of reach from all negativity. Your spiritual armor is tailored and secure. You are safe from corruption. And You are not alone.

PURPOSE IN PRACTICE

- We are influenced by the company we keep. Be intentional about who you allow in your inner circle, and don't be afraid to change their position as your needs and boundaries change.
- If you leave food out too long, it will spoil. Similarly, your dreams are likely to wither if you leave them unprotected.

- Your best ideas should not be passed around like free samples. That's what mall food courts are for!
- What values and aspirations are on your top shelf? Take some time to write down what you cherish the most and how you intend to keep it out of reach of negative influences.

Chapter Twelve

The Great Physician

"I have heard your prayer and seen your tears; I will heal you." ~ 2 Kings 20:5, NIV, abbreviated

MY PATH MADE CLEAR

I 've been thinking about this book for years. I never had it perfectly titled, and I didn't have all the chapters outlined. But I had a vision. I knew I had a message to share with the world. A message of healing and restoration. A message about how we can use our divine gifts and live with purpose as God leads. I am deeply grateful that you have chosen to walk this path with me. I celebrate you for all that you are and all that you are becoming.

And if you will indulge me for one more chapter, I would like to share a few more thoughts on the spiritual aspects of this journey and introduce you to the Great Physician. I pray that you are inspired by these words.

I never would have predicted that this journey would start with a chance meeting with a 70-year-old female minister from Alabama. We haven't met in person, but I read her book, and we traded emails after I finished it. Her name is Edwene Gaines. Her book, *The Four Spiritual Laws of Prosperity,* was truly life-changing for me. I began reading her book in November 2018 and quickly implemented the principles she set forth. I started tithing, setting goals, practicing forgiveness, and leaning into my divine purpose.

It was magical.

My problems didn't go away immediately, but I started to change.

My anxiety decreased, I became more hopeful, and things began to make more sense in my job and in my marriage. I became inspired, and my mind filled with God-given ideas. I began to manifest things I desired as I wrote them down, believed in them, and took action. I can see now that God was waiting for me to reconnect with my divine purpose, and this book was birthed through that process.

I wrote my goals in a notebook. They included many of my wants and some of my needs. I didn't feel guilty for being materialistic. I gave myself permission to enjoy the process and have some tangible rewards to attain along the way. In many ways, we have to incentivize our own success. As Reverend Gaines suggested, I read my goals three times every morning and night. I set a reminder on my phone so that I wouldn't forget. I was committed to giving my best effort.

One of my goals was to attend an Ohio State football game with my dad. He is an alumnus of the school and a huge Buckeye fan. I remember attending a few games as a kid, but it had been at least 15 years since the last one. I realize that as I get older, there are more demands on my time, and I have to prioritize planning ahead for things I value. This was something I really wanted to do. On December 8, 2018, I received a text message from my oldest brother asking if my other brother and I wanted to go to The Rose Bowl in January as a gift to my dad. Ohio State was slated to play against University of Washington. My oldest brother said he would take care of the tickets and I just had to get to Pasadena and make my hotel reservation.

I couldn't believe it! Here I was, not even two weeks from when I wrote down this goal, with an opportunity in my hand. I told my wife, and she agreed this was "a sign" and said I should go. My wife and I hadn't exactly budgeted for the trip, but I knew I was supposed to be there. This was exactly what I asked for. I had to be there. On January 1, 2019, I flew to Los Angeles and started the new year with my father and oldest brother at The Rose

Bowl. And as fortune would have it, Ohio State was victorious. But, more importantly, my faith was made manifest, and I was grateful that God cared about "the little things" in my life, too.

THE POWER OF WORDS

In his book, *The Four Agreements*, Don Miguel Ruiz sets forth a principle: "Be impeccable with your word." It is the first and most powerful agreement. Say what you mean, and mean what you say. The truth is that the words we speak have power. Our words can manifest things in our lives. Don Miguel advises staying away from speaking negatively about ourselves or gossiping about others. Our words should always be in line with truth and love. God created the Universe through His words.

> **God's words are intentional and life-giving.**

He will never stray from what He said and what He promised.

God knows our disease, and He is the Source of our healing. He knows what is best for us because He created us. He designed each of us uniquely and purposely. We wouldn't be here otherwise. We each have an intrinsic set of gifts that are specific to our life path. But we can only complete this path successfully if we maintain a relationship with our Source. Our health depends on it, and

He is our physician. This journey will require us to keep our "appointments" with God, ask Him clarifying questions, and follow His recommendations. We have identified parallels to the practice of medicine throughout this book. We know that prescriptions come from physicians. We put our trust in the physician writing the prescription because we believe they know what they are doing. We assume they are knowledgeable, have the requisite training and skills, and, most importantly, that they care for us. We believe they have good intentions and have sworn an oath not to harm us. We trust they are making their best effort to help us, to act in our best interest.

All of these same attributes define God.

And He is so much greater than what we can define.

He has the training. He has passed all the tests. His thoughts are unsearchable, and His ways are above our ways. There is no other being in the Universe that could do more than God has done, is doing, and will do for us.

Firstly, our Creator does not want to harm us. He is not punishing you or causing you to suffer. He absolutely wants to see you excel, thrive, and live in a state of prosperity and abundance. But you may have to change your expectations and expand your definitions of what this may look like. I did. I thought abundance was only in the form of money. I was limiting myself and my blessings—and I didn't even realize it. Now, I seek abundance in many things: kindness, clarity, optimism, generosity, and connection. I am more prosperous now than at other times when I had more money in the bank.

CUSTOMIZED DELIVERY

Imagine you're getting a prescription filled at the pharmacy. Historically, prescriptions were written on paper, but nowadays, it is just as common to send them in electronically or call them in to the pharmacy. After a prescription is received, the pharmacist reviews and confirms the prescription, counts the appropriate number of pills, and dispenses them for the patient to pick up. The person picking up the prescription has to provide identification and arrange payment when they arrive to retrieve their medication. There is a detailed process to this transaction.

In the same way, God provides His instructions to us through a variety of ways. Sometimes it's through inspired works of writing. Sometimes He may send a message through another person you encounter—a meaningful conversation with a friend, something you learn in class, or a discussion at work. Sometimes He'll plant an idea directly in your mind, or give you a "gut feeling," which is a spiritual intuition. Or perhaps you have a recurring dream, or you keep hearing the same word over and over again through different songs or forms of media. That is no coincidence.

> **God will get His message to you by any means necessary.**

We have to raise our awareness and set aside time each day to search and understand what He is saying to us.

There are no limits to how God can reach you. He will speak to you in a way that you can hear. He's a God of order and clarity. He's not going to make His message confusing or obscure on purpose. We confuse ourselves when we cloud our minds with distractions, negative self-talk, and limiting beliefs. It is our job to quiet our minds and listen. Once we get rid of the noise, God's voice will come through more clearly.

Providing a prescription to a patient is not a random event. Physicians don't close their eyes and throw darts at a "medication wheel of fortune" and see where it lands. The process is much more specific and intentional. They tailor the prescription to the patient's needs. Doctors consider factors like affordability, potential side effects, interactions with other medications the patient may be taking, the patient's medical history, and so forth.

I'm here to suggest that God is even more specific in His prescriptions for us. He knows all the fine details, even the ones we are not aware of, and takes all of them into consideration. None of His prescriptions are intended to harm us, see us fail, or suffer. But we have to follow the instructions on the bottle and use it correctly. If we go our own way, we run the risk of damaging ourselves. And just like any other doctor–patient relationship, we only get refills when we keep our follow-up appointments. This is a relationship. God wants to heal us. He wants to be our Great Physician. It's okay to ask Him questions and get clarification when we are confused or skeptical. We may have doubts that these prescriptions will really do what we hope. God understands our doubts and knows that we're human. But He asks for our trust anyway. Our healing lies at the intersection of His grace and our faith in action.

LIVING YOUR PURPOSE

Evidence of a creative Source is all around us—from the stars in the sky to the waves in the ocean. God has inspired men and women since the dawn of time to enact His plans with purpose. Cities have been built, technology has flourished, and nature evolves every day through divine activity.

How much more can God then help each of us with our routine problems?

All we are required to do is exercise faith.

Think on that word: *exercise*. It's an active word. Faith is not a passive process in which we just sit still and believe. We have to *move* on faith, *act* on faith, and sometimes take a giant *leap* of faith. It would be futile if we brought our prescriptions home from the pharmacy and just left them on the bathroom counter unopened. The medication only works when we take it.

The same thing goes with this journey of self-discovery and growth. It only works as much as we work. And I realize the plan isn't always clear. As much as I would appreciate hearing God's voice audibly, it hasn't happened. I have never had a "Behold, my dear child. Here is the path of your life, in full detail with footnotes" type of encounter with God. But I can usually discern the next step when I listen intently and trust the inner wisdom that He placed inside me.

One of the best pieces of advice I received from an instructor during residency training was:

> **We don't have to figure out what we want to do the rest of our lives; we just have to decide what we want to do *next*.**

It really is one step at a time. We make the next best decision, then the next one after that, then the next one. It's okay to pivot or change course down the road. Don't feel compelled to commit beyond the next decision. God is our Light, and our path is illuminated as we take Him with us. Please hold this truth close to you at all times.

I pray that you have experienced God as you have taken this journey with me. He is calling you and has awakened a spirit of purpose in you as you read this.

Please listen as He leads. Follow the path that has been predestined for your success. This world needs what you have to give. We are depending on you. I am depending on you. God loves you more than you can imagine. And We are never alone. Amen.

About the Author

Adam Meadows, MD is a Board-Certified Psychiatrist and expert on mental health and wellness practices. Through the practices of acceptance and validation, he consistently receives stellar marks in patient satisfaction from individuals he works with. He has been featured on podcasts promoting wellness and was a guest expert on a local news affiliate in Atlanta, GA sharing tips for dealing with holiday stress. Over the past three years, Adam has been invited as a keynote speaker for several employee development workshops ranging from healthcare organizations to the manufacturing industry. The workshop themes centered around poignant titles such as: *When Change is the Only Constant, We Will Make This Climb Together,* and *Entering a New Season.* In 2017, Adam moderated a panel discussion entitled Turning Pain into Passion during a youth symposium hosted by celebrity entertainer, Usher. He currently resides in Atlanta, GA.

9 781642 798494